The Georgia Gold Rush

Gordo - Hope you find gold
in Georgia - *[signature]*
[signature] Susan

[signature]

THE GEORGIA GOLD RUSH

Twenty-Niners, Cherokees, and Gold Fever

David Williams

UNIVERSITY OF SOUTH CAROLINA PRESS

Copyright © 1993 University of South Carolina

Published in Columbia, South Carolina, by the
University of South Carolina Press

First Published 1993
Reissued in Paperback 1995

Manufactured in the United States of America

00 99 98 97   5 4 3 2

ISBN 1-57003-052-9

Library of Congress Catalog Card Number 92–28653

For "T"

Contents

Illustrations

Figures

following page 48

Benjamin Parks, one of the original twenty-niners
First evidence of a gold strike in Georgia
Gold miners in nineteenth-century Lumpkin County
John Ross, principal chief of the Cherokees
Major Ridge, leader of the "treaty faction"
Congressman David Crockett of Tennessee
President Andrew Jackson as "King Andrew the First"
George Gilmer, governor of Georgia (1829–31, 1837–39)
Wilson Lumpkin, governor of Georgia (1831–35)
Drawing tickets in the Land Lottery
Panning for gold on Long Branch
An African-American miner operating a cradle rocker
Bill and Tom Jenkins at their sluice box
The hollow gum rocker or Long Tom
A variation on the sluice box
A variation on the gum rocker and sluice box

following page 112

A two-man dredge boat
Bracing a mine tunnel
Entrance to a gold mine in Lumpkin County
Gold-bearing quartz vein at the Hamilton Mine
A nineteenth-century stamp mill
A small stamp mill
Runaway slave notice
The Federal Branch Mint at Dahlonega
The Cherokees on the Trail of Tears
Matthew Stephenson, assayer at the Dahlonega mint
Nineteenth-century Dahlonega
Hydraulic Mining on Crown Mountain

The Dahlonega Consolidated Gold Mining Company
Stamp mill of the Dahlonega Consolidated
Auraria today
The old Graham Hotel in Auraria

Maps

Preface

It was during my undergraduate days at North Georgia College that I first became aware of the Georgia gold rush. As a native of south Georgia's coastal plains, I was fascinated by the north Georgia mountains. As a student of history, I was intrigued by their past. That past, I found, was laced with tales of the native Cherokees and gold. I spent weekends roaming the hills and canoeing the rivers of the gold region, all the while taking in the natural beauty and trying to imagine what life in these hills must have been like for the Cherokees and the gold miners. I even found a little gold myself on occasion. More difficult to find, however, was a convenient source of information on Georgia's great antebellum gold rush.

For all the popular interest in Georgia's gold rush, "bibliography of the Georgia gold era is," as one Georgia historian recently put it, "thin indeed." A few county histories provide some treatment of gold mining, especially Andrew Cain's *History of Lumpkin County.* But *The Gold of Dahlonega,* a beautifully illustrated work by Lou Harshaw, and *Gold Fever,* companion volume to the Georgia Department of Natural Resources video of the same title, have until now stood alone as attempts to deal with the gold rush in a general way. However, both works are very brief (fewer than fifty pages of text each) and serve as little more than introductions to the topic. The only other books on Georgia's gold rush era are E. Merton Coulter's *Auraria: The Story of a Georgia Gold-Mining Town,* Clair Birdsall's *The United States Branch Mint at Dahlonega,* and Sylvia Head and Elizabeth Etheridge's work *The Neighborhood Mint: Dahlonega in the Age of Jackson.* Coulter's work, still the best portrait of a single mining community, treats only a one-year period between 1833 and 1834 when the town's newspaper, *The Western Herald,* was in publication. The other two books are, like Coulter's, limited in scope, dealing only with the Dahlonega mint. The following pages represent an effort not only to expand on this valuable body of work, but also to bring together and place in perspective all the diverse elements that contributed to this exciting and, in many ways, tragic episode of American history.

This effort would not have been possible were it not for the contributions of those who helped lay its foundations and those who encouraged it along the way. First I wish to thank my parents, Harold and Anita Williams, for their loving support over the years. The support and interest of my in-laws, Donald and Peggy Crisp, is greatly appreciated as well. I also wish to extend affectionate gratitude to those who made my time in Dahlonega such a special experience—Lisa Stepancic, Kay (Ray) and Tom Amsler, Bob Patterson, B. J. (House) Morris, Beth (McNeil) and Robert Abernathy, Kathy (Yarbrough) Jones, Connie Dunbar, Renee (Bruce) Bishop, Debbie (Brannon) Muller, and my brother Scott. For their camaraderie through graduate school, a warm "thank you" goes to Gene Smith, Jim Segrest, Bill Bryant, Susan and Johnny Dollar, Martha and Tim Viator, Sandra and Jack Bergstresser, Mickey Crews, Hal Parker, Church Murdock, Kim Cantrell, and Mary Lee Carter.

I also wish to extend my appreciation to the manuscript readers at Auburn University, whose suggestions were invaluable: Donna Bohanan, Joe Harrison, Tom Belser, Allen Cronenberg, John Cottier, Robert Overstreet, and Robert Cook. Special appreciation goes to Frank L. Owsley, Jr., who directed this work in its original form as a doctoral dissertation.

Thanks for their encouragement and assistance with research go to Ray Rensi of North Georgia College; John Inscoe and Sheree Dendy of the *Georgia Historical Quarterly;* Sharon Johnson of the Dahlonega Courthouse Gold Museum; the Auburn University Department of History; the staff of the Auburn University Library; the staff of the University of Georgia Library; the staff of the Georgia Department of Archives and History, especially Gail Miller; the Georgia Historical Society; the Valdosta State University Research Fund; and Joe Tomberlin and my collegues at the Valdosta State University Department of History. I particularly wish to thank Richard Porter, chief photographer and photo editor of the *Tifton Gazette,* for his help with the illustrations.

Finally, I want to thank my wife Teresa, who has been with me since we met at Dahlonega. Without her constant support and sacrifice, this book might never have been written.

Portions of the book were previously published and appear courtesy of the periodicals indicated: "Origins of the North Georgia Gold Rush," *Proceedings and Papers of the Georgia Association of Historians* (1988); "Gambling Away the Inheritance: The Cherokee Nation and Georgia's Gold and Land Lotteries of 1832–1833," *Georgia Historical Quarterly* 73 (Fall 1989); "Thar's Gold in Them Thar

Hills: The Georgia Gold Rush," *Mountaineer Times* (Summer 1990); "Gold Fever, the Cherokee Nation, and the Closing of Georgia's 'Frontier,' " *Proceedings and Papers of the Georgia Association of Historians* (1990); "Georgia's Forgotten Miners: African-Americans and the Georgia Gold Rush," *Georgia Historical Quarterly* 75 (Spring 1991).

The Georgia Gold Rush

Introduction

"What dost thou not compel the human heart to do, accursed greed for gold?" So wrote the Roman poet Virgil over two thousand years ago. Since the dawn of recorded history mankind has found a special fascination for the precious yellow metal. As Virgil lamented, gold historically has been placed above all else, even human life. In their quest for this lifeless element people have stolen it, lied for it, even killed for it. Entire nations have gone to war for it. Shakespeare called it the worse poison to men's souls. Chilon, a philosopher of the sixth century B.C., observed that "gold is tried with the touchstone, men by gold." The passage of time has seen little change in what is, with some degree of irony, called civilization. The ultimate worth of a human being is still measured more by wealth than by anything else.

But there was a time before the rise of civilizations, even before the first small farming communities had come into being, when people placed little or no value on gold. For tens of thousands of years before the development of agriculture and civilization humans lived as nomadic hunter-gatherers.[1] Constantly on the move, these people knew nothing of working metal. To them stone for making projectile points and other tools was the most important resource provided by nature. Gold, often found remarkably pure in its natural state, is soft and pliable. It is dense but will not hold a sharp edge. Thus it was not of much use to Paleolithic peoples. Nonetheless it seems that this unusual glittering substance held special attraction as a curiosity even then. Small nuggets have been found in caves inhabited by humans dating back forty thousand years.[2]

Mankind's consuming passion for gold dates from a time just before the rise of that complex ordering of human society and interactions we of the modern world call civilization. About five thousand years ago in the region of the eastern Mediterranean Sea there arose a myriad of civilizations and religions that held the sun as their primary object of worship. The pharaohs of ancient Egypt were believed to be direct descendants of the sun god. Ancient writings reveal that gold, because of its amber glow, was thought

1

to have emanated from the sun itself. As late as the first millennium B.C. the Greek poet Pindar referred to gold as the child of Zeus. The Hindus of India viewed gold as "the mineral light," representing divine intelligence. The Christian Book of Revelation describes heaven as a city made of pure gold. Small wonder that gold has come to be widely revered above all other elements.

Gold is indeed a gift of the heavens, though not in quite the way believed by the ancients. It is produced in the fireball of exploding red-giant stars called supernovae. Near the end of its life a massive star larger than our own sun uses up all the hydrogen which fuels the solar fusion process. It then begins to use the helium produced over billions of years of fusion reaction as fuel. This burning produces heavier elements such as carbon and oxygen that are in turn consumed when the helium is exhausted. Most of these elements escape into space as the star swells to many times its original size. The process continues with the star producing increasingly heavier elements until, with a final catastrophic explosion, it creates extremely dense elements like lead, silver and gold. These, along with the previously fashioned elements, are thrown off into the cosmos to become the raw material for the formation of new suns and solar systems. Such stellar debris went into the makeup of our own planetary system nearly five billion years ago.

Volcanic activity spanning hundreds of millions of years, coupled with the tectonic pressures of continental drift, pushed gold and other more abundant metals near the surface of our planet, filling cracks and fissures in the Earth's crust. No one can be certain how much gold lies beneath the surface, but all that has been mined to date would equal almost three billion troy ounces. This is roughly equivalent to a cube measuring 55 feet on each side.

Volcanic and tectonic activity is associated with the formation of great mountain ranges, and gold is occasionally deposited in or near them. The Appalachian chain, born in the formation of the Pangaean supercontinent some three hundred million years ago, experienced just such a boon of nature. The gold veins that were laid down with these Blue Ridge Mountains form an intermittent belt just east of the range and roughly parallel to it, stretching from central Alabama, through Georgia and the Carolinas, northward into the middle states, New England, and Nova Scotia.[3] The belt's richest portion lies in its southern half, and one of its points of highest concentration is the Dahlonega Belt of northeast Georgia.

The soft rolling hills of the Dahlonega gold region were once much taller than they are today. Three hundred million years of erosion have worn the mountains down and molded them into their present configurations, in the process carrying flakes and nuggets of gold to the valleys below. As one mining engineer put it, "only the roots of once mighty veins are left."[4]

Tiny bits of gold that did not sink to the bottom of mountain streams were eventually washed to the sea where they were distributed throughout the oceans of the world. In our epoch a cubic mile of sea water contains about 50 pounds of gold, or 240 million dollars' worth at 400 dollars an ounce. But with current technology the cost of extraction renders the process impractical. More money would be spent obtaining the gold than would be made in the effort.

Larger particles of gold settle in pockets and layers on the valley floors to become placer deposits that can be washed out and collected with shovel and pan. The discovery of such deposits has led to several gold rushes in American history. Almost anyone having even a casual acquaintance with America's past is familiar with the gold rush fame of South Dakota's Black Hills, Colorado's Pike's Peak, Alaska's Klondike, and the California gold region. The latter is more widely known and is generally assumed to be the first area of the country to see a rush of gold fevered prospectors. But though the California gold rush of 1849 was the more famous, it was not the first.

In the middle and late 1820s a series of gold strikes from Virginia to Alabama caused such excitement that thousands of miners from all over the country poured into the region. This Southern gold rush—the first in American history—lasted well into the 1840s.[5] Since the region of northeastern Georgia that would later be called the Dahlonega Belt was one of the richest parts of the gold formation, it was to this area that many of the miners came. So struck were these Georgia miners with that peculiar disease known as "gold fever" that it persisted long after the gold rush was over, and many area residents remain infected to this day.

Unfortunately for the native Cherokees, the gold fields lay on and adjacent to their land—land that Georgia claimed as its own. That claim went back to 1732, when Georgia was granted a colonial charter, and 1763, when the western boundary was fixed at the Mississippi River. But soon after the Yazoo land fraud in 1795, Georgia gave up title to what are today Alabama and Mississippi in exchange for a promise from the federal government to remove Indians occupying the state's remaining claims. According to the agreement, Indian lands were to be "peaceably obtained on reasonable terms."[6] By 1826 the Creek Indians had been forced out of the potentially rich cotton land in what is today southern and western Georgia. The state next turned its attention northward to the Cherokees. The Cherokee Nation had long recognized the threat from Georgia and assisted the Creeks in their struggle against removal. Now the Cherokees faced Georgia alone. This time the driving force behind removal would not be cotton, but gold.

The first gold mines in north Georgia opened in the summer of 1829, and by autumn the region was flooded with gold-hungry prospectors. These Georgia twenty-niners represented only the first wave of an invasion that gathered momentum with lightning speed. Georgia quickly extended its control over the territory, and in 1832 and 1833 the greater portion of the Cherokee Nation, which lay within Georgia's claim, was raffled off in a land lottery from which the Indians themselves were barred. The Cherokees resisted this land grab through the judicial system, and their position was upheld by the United States Supreme Court in the case of *Worcester v. Georgia*. But Georgia, with the backing of President Andrew Jackson, simply ignored the ruling and continued its intrusion of Cherokee land. By 1839 the Cherokees had been driven west on the Trail of Tears to what is today the state of Oklahoma. Nearly every American history text mentions the now famous *Worcester* case and the Trail of Tears, but gold as a motivation for Cherokee removal is often ignored.

Ironically, the gold rush era survived the Cherokees in Georgia by only a few years. The early 1840s saw a dramatic decline in the fortunes of the Southern gold region. It became increasingly difficult for individual prospectors and mining companies to turn a profit. The conclusion was inescapable—the Southern gold fields were beginning to play out. When word of a new gold strike in California reached the miners, they wasted no time in following the banished Cherokees beyond the Mississippi. It was in fact the gold miners of the South who formed the core of the California "forty-niners" and provided the expertise and technological know-how gained during a quarter century of mining Southern gold. As one miner put it, the Southern gold region was "the cradle . . . in which the California '49er was born."[7]

But gold fever never died out in what one resident once called "this favored region of God's creation."[8] Gold mining as a means of making a living, or at least of supplementing a farm income, continued in the Georgia hills through the Great Depression of the

1930s. There was even a second gold rush at the turn of the century that saw the establishment of the largest gold processing plants ever built east of the Mississippi River. But despite the persistence of gold fever and continued high hopes for big strikes, the transformation of this region brought on by Georgia's great antebellum gold rush will never be seen again.

Chapter One

"No Talke, No Hope, Nor Worke, But Dig Gold":
The Origins of Southern Gold Fever

As the story goes, on a crisp autumn day in the Georgia mountains young Benjamin Parks was returning home from a "lick log" on the western side of the Chestatee River where he and his friend, Lew Ralston, provided salt for their livestock. The deer were in abundance this time of year, and "Uncle Benny," as he was known to the locals in later years, strolled quietly through the woods hoping to catch sight of meat on the hoof. While lost in daydreams of venison he accidentally kicked up an unusual stone. The color of this otherwise common stone caught his attention and he paused for a closer look. As he knelt and held the rock in his hand, its true nature suddenly became clear to him. Years later he would remember that the color was something like that of an egg yolk—a deep rich yellow hue. It was gold.[1]

Benjamin Parks was not the first to be captivated by the luster of gold in the southern Appalachians. The original inhabitants of this region were descendants of nomadic hunter-gatherer bands from Asia who migrated to the Western Hemisphere perhaps fifteen thousand years ago across a land bridge that existed between Alaska and Siberia during the last ice age.[2] These first Americans found gold attractive as jewelry, and adornments were often used as items of trade in an extensive network that included almost all of the present-day United States. However, there is no evidence that Native Americans ever mined large amounts of gold. The yellow metal did not have the same power over these people that it had over later generations of Europeans and their progeny.

The first Europeans to touch the shores of North America in search of gold were the Spanish. In 1513 Ponce de León was informed by the Florida natives of a land to the north where gold could be found in abundance, but there is no record to suggest that

7

he made use of this information. It seems that he was much more interested in the immortal promise of the mythical Fountain of Youth, reasoning perhaps that if he found the latter there would be plenty of time to acquire the former.[3]

The first real evidence of gold in North America came to the Spanish in 1516 when the adventurer Diego Miruelo was presented with a small quantity of gold in trading with the Floridians.[4] Three years later the Spanish sea captain Alonzo Piñeda sailed along western Florida and followed the Gulf coast around to what is today Texas. Upon his return he told of rivers containing gold nuggets and natives who wore golden jewelry.[5]

In 1528 the Spanish governor of Florida, Pánfilo de Narváez, landed at Tampa Bay with his army. Despite protests from the natives, Narváez made clear to them that their land was now, as far as he was concerned, the property of the king of Spain. In aggressively exploring his newly conquered lands, Narváez discovered traces of gold among the natives. When asked about its origin, the Indians understandably said it came from a province far to the north called Apalachen. Narváez organized an expedition and set out in search of this land of gold. After several weeks the Spaniards arrived at a village of the Apalachees, a Muskogean people that occupied what is now northern Florida. The intruders searched the entire area but found no gold. It may be that in speaking of Apalachen the natives referred not to the lands at the mouth of the great northern river, the present-day Apalachicola, which is formed by the confluence of the Flint and Chattahoochee, but to the source of the latter in the Appalachian Mountains of north Georgia. If so, this is the first recorded reference to Georgia gold.[6]

The promise of gold lured the Spanish northward, and in 1540 an expedition was organized under the conquistador Hernando de Soto. In his travels through the gold region of the South he heard fantastic tales of people who wore golden hats and of lands where gifts of gold were given in great quantities to women who ruled them. The expedition even came across a young native who showed the Spaniards how gold was mined, melted, and refined by his people. The Spaniards were amazed, and those among them who knew how gold was worked assured the others that this young man had in fact seen gold fashioned "or else the Devil had taught him how. . . . "[7] Some accounts place de Soto in Nacoochee Valley, near the town of Helen in White County, where he was received by the natives with hospitality. But de Soto's quest was in vain, and he died never knowing that the gold he sought had lain just beneath his feet as he traveled through the southern Appalachians.[8]

Inspired by tales of gold related by men who survived the de Soto expedition, Tristán de Luna set out in 1559 to find the source of this gold and to establish permanent settlements. Three hundred Spanish soldiers under Luna's command made their way to the Coosa River, in what is now Alabama, and followed its course into north Georgia. But the expedition was poorly planned and many of Luna's men died of starvation. Some survived only by boiling the leather of their clothes and eating it. By April of 1561 the Spaniards' second great gold-hunting expedition had ended in failure.[9]

More evidence for gold in Georgia was found in 1564 by a French expedition under René Goulaine de Laudonnière during a journey up the Altamaha River. Friendly natives presented the Frenchmen with gold from the Appalachian Mountains, and Laudonnière described how the natives collected it from the creek bottoms: "They draw up sand in a hollow cane-like reed until it is full, then by shaking and jarring it they find grains . . . mingled with sand." The natives also dug pits in the stream beds, collected the sands that fell into them, and panned out the gold.[10]

Other Spanish mining efforts followed and, according to the German traveler Johannes Lederer, Spaniards were operating mines in the southern Appalachians as late as 1670.[11] In 1844 Thomas G. Clemson, a mining engineer and son-in-law of Senator John C. Calhoun of South Carolina, described the remains of an old furnace in Washington County. A small golden button was also found at the site. At Mount Yonah in White County, Clemson found a pair of silver cigar tongs which, he wrote, "are precisely similar to those now used by the Spaniards for holding their 'cigaritos,' or paper cigars."[12]

It is difficult to be certain how much gold the Spanish were able to glean from their workings in what would become Georgia since they did not make their efforts generally known. But it seems evident from the excavations of Spanish mining operations and the tenacity with which they resisted British and French encroachment that the Spaniards clung to the dream of a North American El Dorado for as long as their weakening international position would allow.

The British, though later arrivals, were no less eager in their quest for gold. Their appetite was whetted by Spanish tales of gold in the "New World" and by the evidence of its existence from captured Spanish treasure ships. For the first century of Europe's colonial era Spain ruled the sea lanes between Europe and the Western Hemisphere. Even so, English "sea dogs" like Sir Francis Drake constantly harassed Spanish shipping in the Atlantic. Drake, with his ship *Golden Hind*, prowled the Spanish shipping lanes taking every opportunity to capture galleons laden with gold, silver, and jewels. In 1573 Drake stole an entire Spanish treasure train and four years later engaged in a successful battle with a Spanish treasure galleon, the *Spitfire*. When Drake boarded the ship he found 13 chests of gold coins, 80 pounds of gold ingots, and 26 tons of silver. In 1580 he captured another treasure ship loaded with silver and gold.[13]

Even before the English defeated the Spanish Armada in 1588, they made serious attempts to establish permanent colonies in North America. In 1587 Sir Walter Raleigh made the first such British effort with his Roanoke settlement off the coast of what is today North Carolina. So certain was Raleigh that gold existed in the area that he reserved to himself one-fifth of all precious metals that might be found.[14] But after only two years the colonists disappeared without a trace. To this day the fate of the Lost Colony of Roanoke remains a mystery.

The first successful English settlement at Jamestown nearly failed because of a fruitless gold fever that struck the village in 1608, a year after its founding. According to Captain John Smith, "There was no talke, no hope, nor worke, but dig gold, wash gold, refine gold, load gold." A ship loaded with "yellow dirt" was taken to London, but the cargo was found to be worthless.[15]

Over the next two centuries there was occasional excitement over the prospect of big gold strikes in British North America. Existing evidence suggests that more than a few shafts were sunk in the Carolinas during the colonial period.[16] One account describes a sizable gold nugget taken from the roots of an upturned tree in the Abbeville District of South Carolina sometime before the War for Independence.[17] On Fisher Hill, about six miles south of Greensboro, North Carolina, further evidence of colonial gold mining has been found. There is also a legend that in 1780 an old German miner was frightened off by Cornwallis's troops while working these mines.[18] Thomas Jefferson in his *Notes on Virginia* (1782) told of a piece of gold ore weighing about four pounds that was found on the Rappahannock River. However, none of these eighteenth-century discoveries "panned out." As J. Hector St. John de Crèvecoeur observed in 1793, it would "require the industry of subsequent ages, the energy of future generations, ere mankind here will have leisure and abilities to penetrate deep, and in the bowels of this continent, search for the subterranean riches it no doubt contains."[19]

The first discovery to result in the establishment of permanent mining operations in the United States occurred in 1799 in Cabarrus County, North Carolina, on the property of a farmer named John Reed. Reed's son, Conrad, came across a glittering stone while bow-and-arrow fishing along Little Meadow Creek. It was a heavy lump, about 17 pounds, but the Reeds saw it only as a curiosity and used it as a doorstop. Three years later Reed took the stone with him on a trip to Fayetteville, where, to his astonishment, it was identified as gold ore.[20] Word of the find spread quickly. By 1804 other farmers in western North Carolina had found gold on their own lands, and placer mines were set up. Though placer mining continued over the next two decades, there was no vein mining and no great rush of gold-fevered prospectors. The total amount of gold deposited at the mint in Philadelphia from North Carolina through 1824 was little more than 2,500 ounces valued at just over fifty thousand dollars.[21]

But bigger things were yet to come. A hint of what lay ahead was suggested in an 1825 article, "On the Gold Mines of North Carolina," which appeared in the *American Journal of Science and Arts*. Following an extensive tour of the gold country, Denison Olmsted, a professor of chemistry and mineralogy at the University of North Carolina, offered "some faint hopes of finding the gold in native veins. . . ."[22]

Those hopes were realized later that same year when a farmer and part-time prospector named Mathias Barringer stumbled upon the first gold-bearing quartz vein discovered in North America. While panning along the banks of a small stream in Stanly County called Long Creek, he came to a spot beyond which he could find no gold. The thought struck him that "the gold might have come out of the hill," and he began digging up the slope. To his amazement, Barringer hit a rich vein of gold-bearing quartz which reportedly yielded as much as seventy-five ounces of gold that day. At twenty dollars an ounce, that was around fifteen hundred dollars.[23] By the end of 1825 more than eight hundred ounces from North Carolina had been deposited at the Philadelphia mint, nearly four times the previous year's deposit.[24]

News of Barringer's find spread, and discovery followed discovery in the late 1820s as the gold belt was traced through the

Carolinas northward into Virginia and southward into Georgia and Alabama. One newspaper editor commented in 1829 that discoveries of gold had become so frequent that they were no longer of interest to his readers. He was sure that gold would become as common as lead.[25] Such reports attracted thousands of miners to the Southern gold region, giving rise to America's first major gold rush.

No one is certain when the first discovery of gold was made in Georgia. One account gives the credit to a Cherokee boy who, in 1815, found a nugget while playing along the Chestatee River. He gave the yellow stone to his mother, who wisely concealed the location of this find.[26] Another "first discovery" claim tells of two English miners who in 1823 were traveling as peddlers through McDuffie County, just west of Augusta, and happened to spot a quartz vein rich in gold. They had no money with which to buy the land and as little success in obtaining permission to mine the property. Three years later, so the story goes, they persuaded a wealthy farmer named Jeremiah Griffin to invest in a gold mining venture. Griffin bought three thousand acres of land along the Little River which yielded enough gold to keep up interest in mining the area for many years.[27] However, McDuffie County's was an isolated gold belt 100 miles south of the main gold region that would later come to be known as the Dahlonega Gold Belt.

A still more implausible claim is found in Lucian Lamar Knight's *Georgia and Georgians* (1917). Knight, a Georgia lawyer, minister, journalist, and archivist, tells of a discovery made in 1826 near the town of Villa Rica. For a time, says Knight, Carroll County became "a sort of Klondyke, to which argonauts of the period rushed with pick in hand to unearth the fortunes which they here expected to find."[28] But Knight does not cite the source of this information, and there is no documentary evidence of gold mining anywhere in Georgia before 1829.[29]

These stories and legends of gold strikes in nineteenth-century Georgia cannot be confirmed, nor can they have any claim the be the first. That distinction must go to Native Americans of centuries past. Ozley Bird Saunook, former chief of the Eastern Band of Cherokees, once said that his people knew of gold in the area as early as the sixteenth century when de Soto passed through the region.[30] Other native peoples lived in the southern Appalachians thousands of years before the Cherokees and, though they had little use for it, in all likelihood knew gold was there. Certainly by the nineteenth century the Cherokees knew there was gold on their land, but were understandably reluctant to have that fact generally known. Even so, the secret could not be kept indefinitely. In the late 1820s it became common knowledge that the abundant natural beauty of these Appalachian foothills concealed a more profane wealth.

Long before the white man knew of gold in the region, he coveted the lands of the Cherokee Nation. In the Compact of 1802 Georgia gave up its claim to lands between the Chattahoochee and Mississippi Rivers that are today Alabama and Mississippi. In exchange, the state demanded a promise from the federal government to remove all Indians from its remaining claims "as soon as the same can be peaceably obtained on reasonable terms."[31] The central government agreed to Georgia's terms despite previously having guaranteed Cherokee sovereignty with the Treaty of Hopewell in 1785 and again six years later with the Treaty of Holston.[32]

Georgia's efforts at Indian removal were directed first against the Creeks, who inhabited the potentially rich cotton lands in the southern and central parts of the state. Despite forced land cessions in 1814, 1818, and 1821, the Creeks refused to be driven from their homes without a fight. In May of 1824 the Council at Tuckabatchee resolved that not another inch of ground would be given up to Georgia.[33] One reason for the Creek action was the unwillingness of Anglo-Americans to see the aboriginals as anything other than savages. George M. Troup, governor of Georgia, refused to consider the possibility that Indians would ever be assimilated as citizens on an equal footing with whites. The best they could hope for, said Troup, was a status similar to that of semi-free African Americans. As such, Native Americans would not be allowed to vote, hold public office, bear arms, testify in court against a white person, or send their children to public schools.[34]

In spite of the official Creek policy of resistance to Georgia's land grab, Chief William McIntosh, one of the principal Creek headmen and half-Scot first cousin of Governor Troup, continued without authority to negotiate land cessions with the state. His impertinence led the Creek Council to strip McIntosh of all authority, but still McIntosh refused to desist. As a demonstration of his contempt for the Council, McIntosh signed the Treaty of Indian Springs in 1825, which ceded all remaining Creek lands in areas claimed by Georgia. In return for his cooperation, Troup granted McIntosh rich farm land on the banks of the Chattahoochee. But McIntosh would never profit from his betrayal. Just before daybreak on April 30, 1825, his plantation was surrounded by 150 Creek warriors, all residents of the area surrendered to Georgia by McIntosh. They set the buildings afire and flushed the condemned man from his hiding place. As he rushed out of the main house through the smoke and flame, McIntosh was met by a hail of rifle fire. The last orders of the Creek Council concerning McIntosh had been carried out.[35]

Because of the controversial circumstances surrounding its signing, President John Quincy Adams refused to accept the Treaty of Indian Springs and ordered Troup not to begin surveys of Creek land until a new treaty could be negotiated. Adams dispatched General Edmund Pendleton Gaines with federal troops to arrest any official of the state of Georgia who set foot on Creek territory. Troup countered with a threat of secession and civil war. To avoid further trouble, Adams drew up a new agreement with the Creeks in 1826, the Treaty of Washington. The Creeks found this second treaty every bit as objectionable as the first, but without support from the federal government they had little choice but to accept it. The fate of the Creek Nation was now sealed, and Georgians quickly turned their attention northward to the Cherokee lands.[36]

The Cherokees had long viewed the encroachment of the white man with mounting alarm and were determined to preserve what was left of their homeland. Beginning with its first land cession in 1721, the Cherokee Nation was methodically consumed in large bites first by land-hungry colonies and later by the new United States government. First went territory in South Carolina, then western Virginia and Kentucky. Next to go were lands in Tennessee, North Carolina, Alabama, and Georgia. By 1819 the Cherokees had lost 90 percent of their precolonial territory. After the cession of 1819 the Cherokees adopted an official policy of fierce resistance to any further demands for land. No more land cessions were to be made, and no right-of-way for roads, canals, or horse-drawn railways would be granted.[37]

The Cherokees also began to follow a policy of adaptation to the encroaching Anglo-American-dominated world. With 17,000 Cherokees surrounded by almost a million whites in Georgia, Alabama, Tennessee, and the Carolinas, they could hardly do otherwise. They became farmers, merchants, blacksmiths, and carpenters. They built towns and engaged in trade and commerce.[38] Sequoyah, or George Guess as he was sometimes called, developed a syllabary for their language, and on February 21, 1828, the

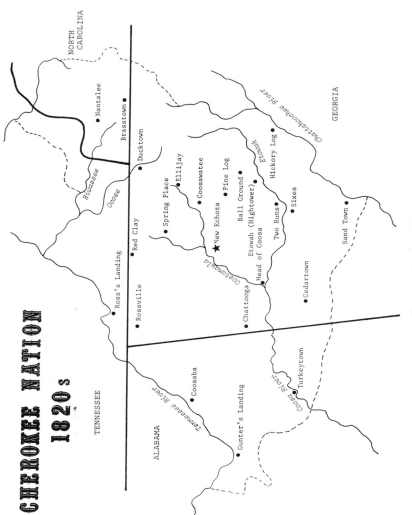

CHEROKEE NATION 1820s

Cherokee Nation, 1820s

NORTH CAROLINA

GEORGIA

TENNESSEE

ALABAMA

Chattahoochee River

Hiwassee

Ocoee

Etowah

Oostanaula

Tennessee River

Coosa River

- Nantalee
- Brasstown
- Ducktown
- Ross's Landing
- Rossville
- Red Clay
- Spring Place
- Ellijay
- Coosawatee
- Pine Log
- New Echota
- Ball Ground
- Etowah (Hightower)
- Head of Coosa
- Hickory Log
- Two Runs
- Sixes
- Chattooga
- Cedartown
- Sand Town
- Coosaba
- Gunter's Landing
- Turkeytown

first issue of the *Cherokee Phoenix* went to press. This newspaper was printed in both English and Cherokee.

The Adams administration provided funds "to promote Indian civilization and education" and declared the Cherokees "citizens of the United States."[39] Various Christian denominations sent missionaries into the Cherokee country to set up churches and schools.[40] And on July 26, 1827, the Cherokees adopted a governmental structure modeled after the U.S. Constitution with New Echota their capital. They even adopted the Old South's symbol of economic power and social status—the institution of slavery.[41]

Elias Boudinot, soon to become editor of the *Cherokee Phoenix,* stressed the "rapidly improving" condition of the Cherokee Nation with statistical evidence. "In 1810 there were 19,500 cattle; 6,100 swine; 1,037 sheep; 476 looms; 1,600 spinning wheels; 30 waggons; 500 ploughs; 3 saw-mills; 13 grist-mills &c. At this time [1826] there are 22,000 cattle; 7,600 horses; 46,000 swine; 2,500 sheep; 762 looms; 2,488 spinning wheels; 172 waggons; 2,943 ploughs; 10 saw-mills; 31 grist-mills; 62 Blacksmith-shops; 8 cotton machines; 18 schools; 18 ferries, and a number of public roads."[42] Such figures attested to the economic vitality and, by nineteenth-century Anglo-American standards, "civilized" state of the Cherokee Nation. But in spite of all this, many Georgians continued to insist that the Cherokees "remained ignorant savages, notwithstanding the constant efforts to change them into better beings."[43]

The Cherokees recognized that their position was precarious at best. As the young John Ridge wrote, "It is true we enjoy self government, but we live in fear, and uncertainty foretells our fall. Strangers urge our removal . . . They point the way West and there they say we can live happy. Our national existence is suspended on the faith and honor of the United States alone. We are in the paw of a Lion—convenience may induce him to crush [us] and with a faint struggle we may cease to be!"[44] The prophetic nature of Ridge's statement would all too soon be revealed.

In December of 1826 the Georgia state senate passed a resolution requesting that the president take steps to initiate a treaty with the Cherokees, "the object of which shall be to extinguish the title to all or any part of the lands now in their possession within the limits of Georgia."[45] The federal government was reluctant to act on Georgia's request since it was bound by previous treaty obligations to protect the Cherokees from further white encroachment. The Compact of 1802 stipulated that any lands granted by the Cherokees must be "peaceably obtained," and they had no intention of giving up their nation without a struggle.

To further clarify its position, Georgia's senate passed a series of resolutions in December of 1827 stating that the Cherokee constitution was "inconsistent" with the rights of Georgia and that the state's General Assembly had all authority to claim title to Cherokee lands "not only upon 'peaceable and reasonable terms,' but upon just such terms as they might [be] pleased to prescribe."[46] This was so, claimed the senate, because prior to the American War for Independence the lands occupied by the Cherokees were part of the British Empire. Georgia argued that the precolonial Indian title to the land was temporary and that they were "mere tenants at will" of the British government. After the defeat of Britain, title of Native American lands passed into the hands of Georgia, and the state "assumed all the rights and powers in relation to the lands and Indians in question, which heretofore belonged to Great Britain." Therefore, said Georgia's senate, the Cherokees were now tenants at will of the state of Georgia and as such might legally be evicted at any time in spite of constitutional guarantees to citizens of the United States against such arbitrary action.[47]

Georgia's resolutions had the desired effect in Washington. Adams now earnestly pressed the Cherokees for a removal treaty. Hugh Montgomery, federal agent to the Cherokees, was instructed to use all his powers of persuasion to wrest such a treaty from them. Montgomery knew the Cherokees would never agree to leave their homeland voluntarily, but, being a Georgian himself, he knew also that the state would be just as persistent in its demands that the Cherokees leave.[48]

At one point the government seemed to be on the verge of a breakthrough. Thomas L. McKenney, director of the Office of Indian Affairs in the War Department, negotiated a removal treaty with a band of about 3,000 Arkansas Cherokees. These Western Cherokees had emigrated at different times since 1790. Some left the East to escape the flood of squatters pushing westward, while others were enticed by federal promises of rich lands in Arkansas. But as far west as these refugees had moved, it was not far enough. By the 1820s land speculators were beginning to press the Arkansas Cherokees. There were too few of them to mount an effective opposition, and the War Department succeeded in coercing them into moving farther west. McKenney felt that the Eastern Cherokees might just as easily be strong-armed into removal after seeing the futility of resistance experienced by their cousins in the West. In a letter to the Reverend Thomas Stuart of Mississippi, McKenney stated flatly, "Indians, I have found, are only children, and can be properly managed by being treated as such."[49] However, the Arkansas Cherokees were despised by the Eastern Cherokees, who saw them as traitors in the struggle against encroachment. Their submission to McKenney's treaty only increased the contempt in which they were held by the Eastern Band. By October of 1828 Montgomery had enrolled only eleven Eastern Cherokees in his removal scheme, and most of these needed money promised by the government to pay off debts. Far from hastening Indian removal, McKenney's treaty served only to make the Cherokees more determined than ever to fight for their homes.[50]

Impatient with federal authorities and alarmed at the entrenchment of the Cherokees, Georgia took matters into its own hands. On December 3, 1828, state representatives introduced a bill in the Georgia General Assembly "to extend the laws of this State over the [Cherokees], and for the purpose of securing to the Indians . . . the enjoyment of civil rights."[51] Two weeks later, the General Assembly enacted a bill mandating the extension of Georgia's authority over the Cherokees. According to the Georgia act, "territory lying within the limits of this State, and occupied by the Cherokee Indians" would be annexed to the counties of Carroll, DeKalb, Gwinnett, Hall, and Habersham on June 1, 1830. After that date, read the act, all laws and customs of the Cherokees would be null and void. The Cherokee Nation, as far as the state of Georgia was concerned, would cease to exist.[52]

This legislative action also proved true to former Governor Troup's earlier prediction concerning the social and legal status of Native Americans. Being "a person of color," no Cherokee or his descendant was considered a competent witness in court cases to which any white person was a party.[53] This allowed for situations in which a white could commit any crime against a Cherokee in the presence of Cherokee witnesses and not be prosecuted. Harsh as it was, the inclusion of this provision in the act is hardly surprising considering the light in which many whites viewed their Cherokee neighbors. George R. Gilmer, who became governor of Georgia in 1829, wrote that "the curious are puzzling themselves with conjectures about the intent of the Almighty in making such beings,—whether they are the descendants of Adam and Eve."[54] In early-nineteenth-century terms Gilmer had brought into question the very humanity of not only the Cherokees, but all aboriginal Americans.

Georgia was encouraged in its actions against the Cherokees by the election in November 1828 of the famed Indian fighter Andrew Jackson to the presidency of the United States. John Quincy Adams and his predecessors had at least paid lip service to the inviolability of treaties with Native Americans, but Jackson was known as a "practical" man who had no patience with such legal niceties as treaty obligations. His inauguration on March 4, 1829, along with the discovery of gold on Cherokee land later that year, marked the beginning of the end for the Cherokee Nation in Georgia and the South.

Chapter Two

"Acting Like Crazy Men":
Gold Fever and the Great Intrusion

In addition to the extension of Georgia's authority over the Cherokees, the late 1820s saw the beginning of the state's antebellum gold mining period. There are conflicting accounts as to who made the discovery that launched the gold rush, and claims to a "first strike" are nearly as unsubstantiated as they are numerous.[1] According to one account, a slave owned by a man named Logan found gold in 1828 along Duke's Creek in what is today White County. Logan and his servant were returning from the gold fields of Rutherford County, North Carolina, when the slave noticed a similarity between the soil of Nacoochee Valley and that of the gold region to the north. He tested a sample and discovered that it indeed contained gold.[2] About the same time another African-American miner is said to have found gold on Bear Creek near the present site of Dahlonega.[3] Another account tells of a man named Jesse Hogan, a prospector from North Carolina, who found gold on a branch of Ward's Creek, also near Dahlonega.[4] Still another gives Pigeon Roost Mine the honor as site of the first discovery of gold. Located just north of Auraria, it was later part of the Barlow mining operations.[5]

Thomas Bowen is supposed to have made yet another discovery on Duke's Creek. Said Judge John Underwood, to whom Bowen related his story, "there came up a storm and blew down some tall timber along Duke's Creek . . . and in the roots of the timber Mr. Bowen found the first gold ever discovered . . . in Georgia."[6] William Blake, the noted geologist and mining engineer, told of another Duke's Creek find in his 1860 report on the Auraria mines of Georgia. According to Blake, a man named John Witheroods (Dahlonega's *Mountain Signal* gave a spelling of "Witherow" in 1874) came across a three-ounce nugget in the little mountain stream.[7] And Benjamin Parks, according to his own account, found gold in 1827 just east of the Chestatee River in what was then Hall County but later became part of Lumpkin County.

21

These tales concerning the origins of Georgia's gold rush have circulated in one form or another since the early nineteenth century. Most have been recited in scholarly books and articles. Even so, no contemporary documentation has been found to support any of the claims. The closest thing to such evidence comes from an 1833 article by Jacob Peck which appeared in the *American Journal of Science and Arts:* "The discovery of gold in Habersham county has been so recent, no more than two years since, that but little has been done to develop the metals concealed there. A gentleman of the name of Wilhero, made researches by comparing the face of the country and appearance of the branches and streams with the gold section in North Carolina, and found deposits of gold through Habersham and Hall counties, and then discovery followed discovery."[8] Perhaps William Blake's "Witheroods" and the *Mountain Signal's* "Witherow" are later incarnations of Peck's "gentleman of the name of Wilhero," but since none of the writers cite their sources, there is no way to be sure.

The most widely accepted claim to the discovery that started the Georgia gold rush is that of Benjamin Parks. As an old man of ninety-one, "Uncle Benny" told his story to a reporter from the *Atlanta Constitution* in July 1894. The article gives 1827 as the year of discovery, but this could not have been the case since Parks went on to say that the area was being invaded by gold seekers within a few days of his find.[9] There was no such rush until two years later. Furthermore, the land on which Parks said he made the discovery belonged to the Reverend Robert O'Barr, pastor of the Yellow Creek Baptist Church, of which Parks was a member. However, the preacher did not come into possession of that property until July 1828.[10]

The widespread belief that Parks made his find in 1828 comes from Andrew Cain's *History of Lumpkin County.* In his chapter "Gold in the History of Lumpkin County" Cain cites an 1896 Georgia Geologic Survey which gives the time of Parks's gold strike as "early in the year 1828." However, the only evidence for this date given by the authors is that "it is claimed by the people of Lumpkin county. . . . "[11]

A further claim for an 1828 Parks discovery comes from the testimony of a friend of Parks who related the tale to his daughter. Based on this story, a 1985 article in the *North Georgia Journal* by Larry Mitchell assigns the following quote to Parks: "It was my birthday [October 27, 1828], so I'd ought to know. I was following a deer path . . . hoping it wouldn't turn across the [Chestatee] river, for late October is no time for fording. I wasn't walking good as common and was well nigh tired down, for I wore some new birthday boots not yet broke in." Word of the discovery spread quickly and, according to the Mitchell article, Parks himself declared "the to-do that followed was going full steam before ever 1829 was rung in."[12] This claim that the gold rush had begun by the end of 1828 was later supported by testimony attributed by L. L. Knight to two early miners, William Reese Crisson and Joseph Edwards. According to Knight's *Georgia's Landmarks, Memorials, and Legends,* gold was discovered some time before their arrival late that year. But this cannot be taken at face value because, as with his 1826 Carroll County claim, Knight cites no documentary evidence.[13]

In any case, Parks goes on to say that when he made his discovery he asked Reverend O'Barr for a lease on the site. O'Barr, thinking the request a joke, laughed at the very suggestion that gold had been found on his property. But he finally agreed to a forty-year lease whereby he would be paid one-fourth of the gold mined on the property. Parks took on a partner, Joel Stephens, and together they returned to the spot where young Benjamin had first stumbled over the sparkling stone. They turned up a pan full of dirt and to their amazement found it speckled with gold. Parks later recalled, "it was more than my eyes could believe."[14]

Preacher O'Barr was soon convinced that his property indeed contained a treasure horde of gold. The thought that Benjamin Parks was mining this gold made him "the maddest man in the country," and he determined to get the lease back from Parks. When O'Barr offered to buy him out, Parks explained that he did not wish to sell, and even if he were so inclined, his partner would never consent. O'Barr stormed off, yelling to Parks, "You will suffer for this yet."

Two weeks later O'Barr appeared at the mine with three members of his family in tow. As they approached, Parks warned his men to take no offensive action lest they be accused of starting a fight. O'Barr once again demanded the lease, and Parks replied, "If you were to pay me ten times its value, I would not sell it to you." To this, O'Barr shot back, "Well, the longest pole will knock off the persimmon." As he spoke, O'Barr's mother broke the sluice gates and began throwing rocks at one of Parks's men. Her obvious purpose was to make the man aggressive; failing to do so, she burst into tears. As her enraged son rushed at the man, Parks grabbed O'Barr by the collar and flung him back. Finding that physical intimidation was useless, O'Barr swore out arrest warrants on Parks and his entire crew. Still Parks would not sell his lease.[15]

Exasperated, O'Barr sold the lot in January 1830 for $1,600. This was not a bad price considering that he had bought the place only eighteen months earlier for $100. That he was able to get such a price for this land indicates that its value had increased substantially. Unfortunately, there is no way to tell exactly when gold might have been found on the property between July 1828, when O'Barr bought it, and January 1830, when he sold out.[16]

The property eventually passed into the hands of Senator John C. Calhoun of South Carolina, to whom Parks said he finally sold his lease for what he *thought* was a good price. According to Parks, Calhoun soon struck a rich vein and took out 24,000 pennyweight in the first month. "Then," said Uncle Benny, "I was inclined to be as mad with him as O'Barr had been with me. But that is the peculiarity of gold mining. You will go day after day, exhausting your means and your strength until you give it up. Then the first man who touches the spot finds the gold the first opening he makes."[17] This observation on the uncertainty of gold mining is true enough, but Parks's claim to a lease is much less certain. There is no record of the mine's being under lease when Calhoun bought it, and Parks's 24,000 pennyweight figure makes the story even more implausible. A pennyweight is one-twentieth of an ounce. With gold going for $20 an ounce, the find would have been worth $24,000. Calhoun's first deposit at the federal mint in Philadelphia was valued at only $603.93.[18]

Despite the popularity of the Parks legend and the various claims to "first" discoveries between 1826 and 1828, there is no documentary evidence of the discovery of gold in Georgia until August 1, 1829, when the following notice appeared in a Milledgeville newspaper, the *Georgia Journal*:

> GOLD.—A gentleman of the first respectability in Habersham county, writes us thus under date of 22d July:
> "Two gold mines have just been discovered in this county, and preparations are making to bring these hidden treasures of the earth to use."
> So it appears that what we long anticipated has come to pass at last, namely, that the gold region of North and South Carolina, would be found to extend into Georgia.[19]

This is not to say that no one had found gold in Georgia prior to the summer of 1829, but it can be said with certainty that no gold rush was under way before that time. According to the *Macon Tele-graph*, it was not " . . . until the winter of 1829 and 30, when the precious metals having been discovered in great abundance upon our Cherokee soil, great numbers of people from Georgia and other States rushed to the Territory in search of its treasures."[20] Additionally, throughout the late 1820s Georgia newspapers ran articles telling of gold strikes in Virginia and the Carolinas. How-ever, not a word about Georgia gold appears until August 1829. If there had been a gold rush in Georgia before then, the state's newspapers could hardly have ignored it while at the same time reporting gold discoveries in other states.

In the autumn of 1829, articles describing the vast riches of Georgia's gold region began appearing in newspapers across the state, and by the end of that year the Georgia gold rush was well under way. It is difficult to know exactly how many twenty-niners were involved in this early phase of the gold rush, but clearly they numbered in the thousands. *Niles' Register* reported that by June 1830 there were four thousand miners washing the sands near the later site of Dahlonega on Yahoola Creek.[21] Best estimates give the total number of Georgia miners at about ten thousand.[22] As Uncle Benny Parks recalled, "The news got abroad, and such excitement you never saw. It seemed within a few days as if the whole world must have heard of it, for men came from every state I had ever heard of. They came afoot, on horseback and in wagons, acting more like crazy men that anything else. All the way from where Dahlonega now stands to Nuckollsville there were men panning out of the branches and making holes in the hillsides."[23] In a letter to his congressman, Samuel N. Wales of Habersham County wrote that "no event within my recollection has produced so much ex-citement among the people as the discovery of gold."[24]

The twenty-niners who flocked to the Georgia gold fields were a varied assortment of adventurers, but they all had one thing in common—the dream of gold and quick riches. These early days of the Georgia gold rush saw the establishment of shanty towns in which "drinking, gambling and fighting were rife, and the laws were little known and less cared for."[25] The in-habitants had been struck with a disease called "gold fever," which made them, in the words of one writer, "oblivious of duty, forgetful of friends, and even of self and bodily comfort."[26]

Others were even more harsh in their assessment of the char-acter of these men. In his memoirs, Governor George Gilmer wrote this opinion of the twenty-niners:

Many thousands of idle, profligate people flocked into [the gold region] from every point of the compass, whose pent up vicious propensities, when loosed from the restraints of law and public opinion, made them like the evil one in his worst mood. After wading all day in the Etowah and Chattahoochee Rivers, picking up particles of gold, they collected around lightwood knot fires, at night, and played on the ground and their hats, at cards, dice, push pin, and other games of chance, for their day's findings. Numerous whiskey carts supplied the appropriate aliment for their employments.[27]

Another eyewitness recorded that one group of prospectors at the Chestatee Mines "presented a most motley appearance of whites, Indians, halfbreeds and negroes, boys of fourteen and old men of seventy—and indeed their occupations appeared to be as various as their complexions comprising diggers, sawyers, shopkeepers, peddlers, thieves and gamblers, etc. Besides them were also found in the hopeful assemblage two Colonels of Georgia Militia, two candidates for the legislature and two ministers of the Gospel, all no doubt attracted thither by the love of gold."[28] One Georgia judge referred to these men as "thieves, gamblers, and murderers—quarrelsome, drunken and malicious—forming altogether a lawless, ungovernable community."[29]

In overrunning Cherokee lands, certainly these twenty-niners were breaking the law, but they may not have been completely lawless. Some of the old prospectors remembered years later how a kind of vigilante justice operated in the mining camps. William Reese Crisson, one of the original twenty-niners, told of an incident that occurred at Dahlonega some time before 1833 when it was still known as "Headquarters." According to Crisson, when a man called "Long Jerry" stole a fifty-pound barrel of flour, the other miners set the three-foot barrel on a four-foot stump and made the thief climb to the top and stand there for three hours under a blazing sun.[30] On another occasion one of the miners was found with a stolen barrel of whiskey. As Crisson told the story,

Several wagons had drove in about where Dahlonega is now located, being head quarters for the diggins. One wagon drove down on Ducan's Branch in the afternoon, perhaps Thursday, and among the teamster's barrels was a ten gallon keg of extra fine whiskey. Next morning it was missing, and on Saturday morning it was found in a man's tent . . . covered with pine straw and his blankets. The news spread like wild fire that a man had been stealing and that the whiskey was concealed in his tent. By Sunday morning a crowd of several hundred miners had gathered there. The prisoner and keg were brought before the assemblage. Quite a number of men spoke on the case. Some for whipping, some for cropping and branding, and others in favor of banishment. About this time a tall man got up . . . and said: "I wish to make an inquiry before making up my mind—is the whiskey good?" . . . it was. "Let us try some of it," said the speaker. The keg was empty. "Well then I move to fill it up with water and lay it on the prisoner's shoulder and proceed to march to headquarters and thence it be honorably discharged." All agreed that it was legal business, the demonstration of prefered [sic] legality.[31]

Legal or not, the sentiment that the gold region was a "lawless, ungovernable community" was echoed by many who regretted that gold had been discovered in Georgia at all. One writer feared that Georgia might go the way of Spain with its new-found wealth, believing that a flood of gold from Mexico and Peru into Spain had "produced the decline and degeneration of that kingdom, changing the character of its population from the most enterprising to the most indolent in Europe."[32] Similar misgivings were echoed by Caroline Gilman, a visitor to the gold region, who warned that Georgia might, "like Midas, find her wealth a curse, and, losing the habits of regular productive industry, starve in the midst of uncounted riches."[33] The editor of the *Georgia Journal* called it a sad day for Georgia when gold was found in its soil. He further urged the General Assembly to make gold mining illegal in an effort to head off the possibility of a major gold rush. "Those who live to see the result," warned the *Journal*, "will be convinced to their sorrow that this advice is not founded on a slight or partial consideration of the subject."[34]

But the spread of gold fever proved impossible to stop, fueled as it was by daily reports from the mines of spectacular finds.[35] The product of Georgia mines was said by some to be "virgin gold, as pure as that precious metal can be."[36] Others claimed that its purity exceeded that of the famous Spanish doubloon.[37] One newspaper reported that nearly nine thousand dollars' worth of gold was sold in Milledgeville during a three-week period in 1830. This was in addition to an unknown amount that had recently been sold to local jewelers.[38] Athens's *Southern Banner* printed an estimate that during the first nine months of that year, almost a quarter of a million dollars in gold had passed through Augusta.[39]

National newspapers also carried articles describing riches in Georgia that were there for the taking. Some told of nuggets worth anywhere from one to two hundred dollars.[40] One editorial suggested that the Cherokee territory contained more than one hundred million dollars' worth of gold.[41] Another article reported that the miners on Yahoola Creek were panning out ten thousand dollars in gold every day.[42]

Claims were made that a single prospector with no more than a pan and shovel could gather upwards of thirty dollars' worth per day. Actually these early prospectors were fortunate to pan out five dollars' worth of gold a day. The experience of C. P. Gordon was typical. Working one mine over a four-month period, he averaged from one and a half to two pennyweight per day (less than two dollars' worth). One miner wrote to a friend, "You can form no idea of the exaggerated accounts there is reported of this country 80 or 100 miles off. Gold they think can be had, to the satisfaction of avarice itself by a little labour."[43]

Nevertheless, some of the Georgia twenty-niners appear to have done very well for themselves. In November 1829 the *Southern Recorder* reported that four Habersham County workers took an amount of gold worth $270 in a single day out of a mine owned by a "Gen. Cleveland."[44] Another Habersham County mine, which was worked by fifteen hands, produced 1,001 pennyweight, or 50 ounces, in a five-day period. This was believed to be the largest amount of gold ever obtained by so few men in such a short time.[45] Early workings on the Lumsden mine showed it to be a treasure house of diamonds as well as gold.[46] In one of the first vein mining efforts in Georgia, a Mr. Elrod of Hall County, with seven men working his property, made $180 in one day.[47] In 1830 gold was discovered in Carroll County near Villa Rica on Pine Mountain.[48] These new mines had an annual production of more than 25,000 pennyweight.[49]

With thousands of miners at work in the gold fields, some making a good profit, a significant amount of gold was coming out of north Georgia. In 1830 the United States mint at Philadelphia received $212,000 from the Georgia gold fields and by the end of 1832 over half a million dollars' worth had been deposited.[50]

The sudden influx of thousands of twenty-niners into the Cherokee Nation was known even at the time as the "Great Intrusion."[51] Georgia was not to take possession of the area until June of 1830, and even then the Cherokees would retain title to their property until the state decided how to dispose of it. But this slight protection was practically worthless. The General Assembly had seen to it that no white person could be prosecuted for crimes against the Cherokees by stating that an Indian was incompetent to

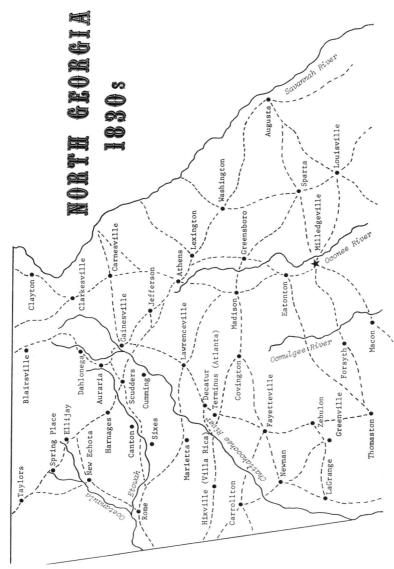

North Georgia, 1830s

bring suit against, or be a witness against, a white person in a court of law.[52] This cleared the way for unchecked abuse of the Cherokees. Thus protected by the state, bands of whites roamed the Cherokee Nation taking not only gold but also livestock, household goods, and anything else they could carry away. Sometimes they shot cattle and horses for fun.[53] In one incident a Cherokee family returned home late one evening to find that all their belongings had been stolen. Even the feather bed was gone.[54]

The natives protested loudly against such injustices. Wrote one aggrieved Cherokee, "Our neighbors who regard no law and pay no respects to the laws of humanity are now reaping a plentiful harvest by the law of Georgia. . . . We are an abused people."[55] But there was little the Cherokees could do. It seemed the more vehemently they protested, the more eagerly the miners came. As the editor of the *Cherokee Phoenix* put it, "Right or wrong, they are determined to take the country."[56]

Benjamin Parks himself lamented the Great Intrusion. When Parks was a child, his family moved from North Carolina to Hall County. They had many Cherokee neighbors and were welcomed among them. According to Uncle Benny, "We always treated them right and they did the same by us." As a young man, Parks often took his meals at the homes of Cherokee friends and came to love a dish that the natives called "conee-banee." He also fell in love with the daughter of a Cherokee chief. In a fond reminiscence of years gone by, he described her as "a stunner—as pretty a woman as I ever saw. Her eyes I can remember yet." His love was shared by the Cherokee maiden, and the two wanted badly to marry. But the prevailing prejudices of the day prevented the union. Within a few years the Cherokees were forced from their homeland, and Benjamin never saw his Indian princess again. Uncle Benny's reaction was described in an article in the *Atlanta Constitution*. The Cherokees, he said, " 'would have gotten on all right if they had been left alone. Those were good times,' soliloquized the old man, as his eyes wandered in their gaze toward the tall tree tops."[57]

Desperate to stem the flow of intruders into their nation, the Cherokees turned to the federal government for help. The federal agent to the Cherokees issued an order for all intruders to cease their mining activities immediately and remove themselves from Cherokee territory.[58] Some miners complied with the government's request to leave, but a far greater number did not. In a letter to the Cherokee agent, one group of Georgia miners conceded that it had been wrong of them to intrude on Cherokee lands in search of gold and that such actions ought to be stopped. These Georgians had left the mines peacefully, but on finding that the government's "reasonable request . . . had not induced the citizens of other States to abandon their searches," they returned to their diggings. However, they insisted that they were ready to leave at any time if others were compelled to do likewise.[59]

To enforce compliance with the order for intruders to abandon their mines, the United States dispatched army regulars. Although this federal force had little success in driving out the gold diggers, Governor Gilmer and the General Assembly howled in protest at the very notion of the U.S. Army's exercising authority within what they considered to be the boundaries of their sovereign state. The Georgians also feared that federal protection might further steel the Cherokees against removal.

In June of 1830 Gilmer issued a proclamation "notifying all persons whom it may concern that the jurisdiction of this State is now extended over all the territory in the occupancy of the Cherokees."[60] In stating Georgia's claim on the Cherokee Nation, Gilmer repeated an earlier proclamation by the state senate in declaring that ownership had passed to Georgia from "the Kings of Great Britain."[61] Neither the senate nor the governor expressed an opinion as to who owned the land before the British kings.

Gilmer immediately wrote a letter to President Jackson informing him of the proclamation and complaining bitterly that the continued presence of federal troops was a violation of the United States Constitution. Since Georgia had formally extended its jurisdiction over Cherokee land, the federal government had no authority there.[62] Jackson was himself an advocate of Indian removal and had only a month before rammed through Congress the hotly-debated Indian Removal Act calling for the relocation of all Eastern tribes to areas beyond the Mississippi River. He complied with Gilmer's request and agreed to withdraw the army.

In addition to announcing Georgia's extension of authority over the Cherokee Nation, Gilmer's proclamation also ordered both intruders and Cherokees to cease their mining operations on land that the state considered its own. Gilmer insisted that such a policy was necessary not only to protect state property but also, in his words, "to put an end to the lawless state of society which has hitherto existed among the gold diggers."[63] In an attempt to give some teeth to the policy, he brought the weight of the state judiciary to bear by appointing a superintendent of public lands "whose business it was to restrain trespassers by writs of the courts."[64] But proclamations and court orders could hardly be expected to succeed where the army had failed. Prospectors simply ignored the state and continued their diggings.

While public opinion ran strongly in favor of Gilmer's effort to restrain the miners, no one was quite sure how this might actually be done. The editor of the *Georgia Journal* suggested that the General Assembly make gold hunting in Cherokee country illegal and provide stiff penalties for violators.[65] However, the *Southern Recorder* warned that such a law "would not, in all probability, be respected."[66] Nonetheless, the General Assembly enacted legislation declaring "that persons guilty of digging for gold . . . unless authorized; and persons not authorized by law, employing white men, Indians, or negroes, in digging gold . . . [were] to be indicted, and if found guilty, sentenced to confinement in the Penitentiary for four years."[67] But, as predicted, the law found very little respect among the miners. Gilmer himself recognized the futility of his attempts to protect the mines and later admitted that he "found paper bullets but light artillery against masses of men who could not read."[68] Lacking authority to send Georgia troops into the region, Gilmer reluctantly acquiesced to the return of the U.S. Army until he was empowered by the General Assembly to raise a force of Georgia men to patrol the mines.[69]

More than three hundred federal troops under the command of Major Phillip Wager passed through Columbus, Georgia, on their way to the gold region in September 1830.[70] The expressed purpose of this expedition was to augment forces already in north Georgia, "displace the gold diggers, and aid the authorities of Georgia in executing the laws of that state over the Cherokee territory."[71] On arriving in the gold region the troops established a station between the Chestatee and Etowah Rivers and began making arrests. Detachments of about twelve men each combed the hillsides and creek bottoms in search of miners. These units set out early in the morning and patrolled an assigned area, returning in the evening with their prisoners. Despite orders from their commanding officers, it is likely that the soldiers took no great pleasure in their duty. Recalled one old prospector, "I do not think the soldiers really desired to arrest the boys; but when they came upon them, they had to do so."[72]

Dawn-to-dusk raids forced the miners to shift their activities from daytime to night. Gangs of intruders crossed the Chestatee River into Cherokee territory every night, filled large sacks with gravel from known placer deposits, and got back across the river before daybreak. The soldiers countered this move by sending out squads with three days' rations to extend the range of their patrols. It was at this point, remembered one miner, that "the boys began to have some fun." Sentinels were placed around the soldiers to keep track of their whereabouts. When these lookouts warned of the army's approach, miners scattered in all directions.[73] On September 20, 1830, Major Wager wrote that as he and his men were closing in on a large mining camp the night before, an alarm was sounded "and hundreds immediately fled to the woods." Even so, the detachment captured more than 200 miners that evening.[74]

Occasionally the army employed Cherokee detachments to supplement its outnumbered forces. In one instance a Cherokee captain by the name of Old Fields was sent to arrest a group of Georgians from Carroll County who entered Cherokee territory not to mine gold but to serve writs on some natives at Hightower. Captain Old Fields delivered the Georgians to federal officers as ordered, and they were promptly released. A suit was filed by the Georgians against Old Fields for false imprisonment. Although the arrests had been ordered by United States Army officers, the helpless Cherokee was forced by the courts to hand over his property in compensation. As the *Cherokee Phoenix* observed, "United States' troops authorized this arrest, and the poor honest Indian had to suffer all."[75]

After arrests were made, the standard procedure was to burn the miners' huts and break up their machinery.[76] At Sixes in Cherokee County one detachment destroyed nineteen buildings on September 26, 1830. The next day this same unit set fire to twenty-two buildings "of good size" at a mining camp called Phillips'.[77]

After their arrests the miners were hastily escorted off Cherokee lands. But no sooner had one group of miners been driven from a choice mining camp than another took its place. In many cases the abandoned workings were taken over by Cherokee gold hunters. This infuriated the former occupants, and they began returning to the mines in droves. In a letter to Governor Gilmer one eyewitness expressed fears that if the Cherokees were not prevented from digging for gold, white mobs might cause bloodshed.[78] At Gilmer's request the army adopted a policy of forbidding anyone, native or intruder, to work the mines.[79] This did little to turn back the flood of intruders and succeeded only in angering the Cherokees. Wrote the editor of the *Cherokee Phoenix*, "It now appears plainly that our *great father* considers us in the light of intruders."[80] In a letter addressed to the commander of the federal troops, one group of Cherokees from "Alatoony" wrote of their brethren at the mines, "They are laboring in an honest way upon their own lands for the support of their families; they intrude upon the possessions of none; they infringe on no one."[81] Notwithstanding Cherokee protests, the arrests of both intruders and natives continued. All the way from Sixes northeast to the Chestatee River, men were rounded up and driven off only to return when their evictors moved on to the next mining site.

As if the Cherokees did not have enough troubles to contend with, there was the additional harassment of the "Pony Clubs." These were bands of white thugs who, like the later Ku Klux Klan, rode nightly across the countryside visiting death and destruction on their helpless victims. Families were driven from their homes, farms were burned, and livestock stolen or killed.[82] In the spring of 1831 Elias Boudinot, editor of the *Cherokee Phoenix*, estimated that these criminals had already made off with around five hundred head of horses and cattle.[83] Occasionally individuals or whole families were murdered as they slept. There was even an attempt on the life of the principal chief of the Cherokees, John Ross.

On the evening of November 30, 1831, a tall, gaunt stranger appeared at the home of Major Ridge, whom John Ross and his brother Andrew were visiting. The man said that his horse had been stolen and asked if anyone had recently crossed Ross's Ferry, for he had tracked his horse to this point. Ross replied that to his knowledge no one had crossed that evening, but offered to help the man find his horse. Later that night John and Andrew Ross met the stranger and his Cherokee guide, Onehutty, near the ferry. Moments later a horseman was sighted on the crest of a low hill and the party gave chase. The man was overtaken and captured with what seemed to Ross curious ease. It quickly became apparent that the supposed horse thief was actually in conspiracy with the stranger to assassinate Chief John Ross.[84]

Without warning, the stranger dismounted and yelled, "Ross, I've wanted to kill you for a long time, and I'll be damned if I don't do it now." John and Andrew instantly wheeled their horses and fled, too quickly for the stranger to fire off an accurate shot. Next morning Onehutty appeared at Lavender's Store with a large bruise on his cheek. The Cherokee, who was unaware of the plot (the Rosses later testified he had been unarmed), said that after the Ross brothers' escape the two white men turned on him. He disarmed the tall stranger, stabbed him in the ribs with his own knife, and escaped into the night. The two would-be assassins were later found to be connected with the Pony Clubs.[85]

These clubs were only one indication of the chaos that reigned in the Cherokee Nation despite the presence of federal troops there. Anxious to calm the situation and to see the U.S. Army replaced by Georgia militia, Gilmer called an early session of the General Assembly.[86] In December 1830 the assembly passed two acts designed to secure the mines and bring order to the gold region. The first officially directed Governor Gilmer to take possession of the mines.[87] The second and more significant act gave teeth to the first. It authorized the creation of a guard of up to sixty men for the purpose of driving intruders from the mines. Each member of this Georgia Guard was compensated "at the rate of fifteen dollars per month when on foot, and at the rate of twenty dollars per month when mounted." To keep the Guard under control, its commander was authorized three sergeants who were paid an additional five dollars per month and empowered to dismiss any man for disorderly conduct. Anyone caught prospecting by the Guard would be subject to the prescribed penalty of four years at hard labor.[88]

However, such a threat did little to deter men skilled in avoiding the army. It was common practice among the miners to post lookouts in the area to warn of the Guard's approach, just as they had done with the federal troops, and then scatter into the surrounding hills when an alarm was sounded. Even when the Georgia Guard succeeded in making arrests, it was often confronted with fierce resistance. One such incident occurred on January 17, 1831. The Guard, under the command of Colonel Charles H. Nelson, had apprehended eleven intruders at the Daniels mining camp. About sixty of the prisoners' friends gathered at Leather's Ford on the Chestatee River where the Guard would cross into Hall County. The group placed obstructions in the river, hid themselves on the opposite bank, and awaited the Guard's approach. As the detachment emerged from the river, it was violently attacked by the miners. According to Colonel Nelson's account, they used "everything except guns" in the assault. However, the Georgia troops would not be intimidated. The Guardsmen fixed bayonets and charged their assailants, sending them flying in all directions. No members of the Guard were injured in the scuffle, which came to be known as the Battle of Leather's Ford, but one miner was seriously wounded, and it was thought that the man might die. But upon examination of his injuries it was discovered, as one militiaman put it, "that he was not likely to experience the fate so richly merited by his infamous life, and still more infamous conduct in this affray."[89]

Feelings ran high on all sides—among the miners, among the Guardsmen, and especially among the Cherokees. It was the Cherokees, after all, who had everything to lose. Andrew Jackson's election to the presidency was only one indication of just how close they were to losing their homes, their land, and, in many cases, their lives. Their already desperate situation would become even more hopeless over the next few years as Jackson, ignoring treaty obligations and the Constitution itself, pressed forward with his Indian removal policy.

Chapter Three

"Get a Little Further":
The Cherokee Nation Abandoned

The election of Andrew Jackson as president in the fall of 1828 all but sealed the Cherokees' fate. Before Jackson took office the Cherokees looked to the federal government and the presidency for protection in the struggle for their very existence. But now with Jackson in the White House, prospects for all Native Americans appeared bleak. It seemed that the Southern nations were to be removed as the result of an election in which they were barred from participation.

In June 1829, only three months after his inauguration, Jackson addressed an open letter to Native Americans. Its use of platitudes and condescension seems strangely familiar to anyone acquainted with modern political rhetoric.

> *Friends and Brothers.* By permission of the Great Spirit above, and the voice of the people, I have been made president of the United States, and now speak to you as your father and friend, and request you to listen. Your warriors have known me long. You know I love my white and red children, and always speak with a straight, and not with a forked tongue; that I have always told you the truth. I now speak to you as my children, in the language of truth—Listen.
>
> Where you now are, you and my white children are too near to each other to live in harmony and peace. Your game is destroyed, and many of your people will not till the earth. Beyond the great river Mississippi . . . your father has provided a country large enough for all of you, and he advises you to remove to it. There your white brothers will not trouble you; they will have no claim to the land, and you can live upon it, you and all your children, as long as the grass grows and water runs, in peace and plenty. It will be yours forever.[1]

Jackson's motives for wanting the Southern Indians moved westward involved much more than a desire to see that his "white and red children . . . live in harmony and peace." Before entering the White House Jackson made a fortune in land speculation. It was his financial ties to other wealthy speculators, along with his fame as the "Hero of New Orleans," that paved the way for his entrance into politics. As president, Jackson maintained a strong association with land speculators. His closest advisors, referred to as the "kitchen cabinet," were men who themselves dabbled in the business or had ties to those who did. The expulsion of not only the Cherokees but all Southern Indians would mean boom times for Jackson and his associates.

In May 1830, just over a year after taking office, Jackson pushed through Congress the Indian Removal Act. This legislation called for the administration to encourage all Eastern tribes to relocate across the Mississippi River. Though Jackson exerted considerable influence over Congress, the act passed only over the objections of a good many senators and representatives. Most of this opposition came from Northern congressmen, but a few Southerners, most notably Representative David (Davy) Crockett of Tennessee, were also against the arbitrary relocation of whole Indian nations to unfamiliar lands. Crockett had fought under Jackson almost twenty years earlier during the Creek Civil War, but had since, like many frontier settlers, gained considerable respect and even affinity for his Indian neighbors. The major push for a general removal of Southern Indians came not from people like Crockett, but from those politically and financially powerful groups that stood to gain most from land speculation.

Chief John Ross knew Crockett to be a reliable friend who would render every possible assistance to the Cherokee cause. Ross had served with Crockett in the Creek Civil War, during which he was a member of Jackson's Cherokee regiment. In a letter to the Tennessee congressman, Chief Ross praised Crockett for his integrity and assured him that "the day of retributive justice must and will come."[2] For his part Crockett had no patience with those who placed political expediency above what he saw as "simple justice."[3] Because of their willingness to heel at Jackson's command, Crockett likened many of his colleagues to canines whose collars bore the inscription "My Dog—Andrew Jackson."[4] In Crockett's words, "It was expected of me that I was to bow to the name of Andrew Jackson, and follow him in all his motions and mindings, and turnings, even at the expense of my conscience and judgment. Such a thing was new to me, and a total stranger to my principles. I know'd well enough, though, that if I didn't 'hurrah' for his name, the hue and cry [would be] raised against me, and I [would be] sacrificed if possible." However, he concluded, "I would sooner be honestly and politically d——nd, than hypocritically immortalized."[5]

The sectional division brought on by this controversy produced some of the most heated debate ever seen in the short life of the American republic. Northern men like Senator Theodore Frelinghuysen of New Jersey, who had a long record of sympathy for the Indians, spoke for three days on the Senate floor in their defense. "We have crowded the tribes upon a few miserable acres of our Southern frontier: it is all that is left to them of their once boundless forests: and still, like the horse-leech, our insatiate cupidity cries, give! give! give!"[6] Representatives of the expansive "slaveocracy" like Senator John Forsyth and Representative Wilson Lumpkin of Georgia responded by accusing their Northern counterparts of hypocrisy.[7] The North, said Southerners, was interested in the welfare of the Indian only insofar as he provided a barrier to Southern expansion. Such expansion would pose a serious threat to the relative Congressional power of the North. Proponents of Indian removal also pointed out that unwanted Indians had long since been driven from areas above the Mason-Dixon Line. According to Forsyth, the thrust of Frelinghuysen's speech was abundantly clear. "The Indians in New York, New England, Virginia, etc., etc., are to be left to the tender mercies of those States, while the arm of the General Government is to be extended to protect the Choctaws, Chickasaws, Creeks and especially the Cherokees from the anticipated oppression of Mississippi, Alabama and Georgia."[8] Lumpkin, who had himself proposed an Indian removal bill three years earlier, invoked the blessings of Providence when he declared that God had formed the Southern frontier "for purposes more useful than Indian hunting grounds."[9]

Despite this regionalism, Crockett was not the only influential Southern friend the Cherokees had. Henry Clay of Kentucky felt certain that if they remained firm in their conviction and persisted in their resistance to removal, the Indians would eventually succeed. "Public opinion is with them," said Clay. "Justice is on their side; honor, humanity, the national character, and our Holy religion all plead for them. With such advocates they ought to prevail, and they will prevail, if their friends are not too inactive."[10] But Clay's influence could not turn the tide of Jacksonian support in Congress. When the Removal Bill finally came up for consideration in the Senate, it passed by a vote of 28 to 19. The margin of victory in the House was an even more narrow 102 to 97.[11]

The only Tennessee vote cast against the Indian Removal Act was Crockett's. In accordance with his earlier prediction, he was indeed politically damned for his opposition to Jackson. Crockett was defeated in his bid for reelection the next year. He made a political comeback and served in Congress from 1833 to 1835, but was again defeated for the next term. This time he was through with politics. Telling the voters of his Tennessee district, "You may all go to hell and I will go to Texas," he set out to start a new life on the frontier.[12] Four months later Crockett died at the Alamo.

As for Georgia, its efforts against the Cherokees now had the sanction of both the executive and legislative branches of the federal government. The only hope for justice left to the Cherokees was the Supreme Court.

After passage of the Indian Removal Act, the Cherokees were flooded with offers from lawyers across the country to form a legal team and prepare a case to take to the federal courts. Such a team was put together with William Wirt of Baltimore at its head. This son of a tavern keeper had won fame more than twenty years earlier as prosecutor in the trial of Aaron Burr and served as attorney general under James Monroe and John Quincy Adams.[13] In addition to Wirt and his team, the Cherokees hired William H. Underwood and Thomas W. Harris to handle local cases arising in Georgia's Western Judicial Circuit, which bordered on the Cherokee Nation. Underwood was a particularly valuable ally to the Cherokees since he had once been a judge of the Western Circuit.[14]

Less than a month after passage of the Removal Act, Wirt addressed a letter to Governor Gilmer in which he outlined the Cherokee position and suggested that Georgia and the Cherokees create a case based on the issue at hand for submission to the Supreme Court.[15] In his response Gilmer expressed puzzlement over why a citizen of Maryland should concern himself with the actions of Georgia's elected officials. Besides, continued Gilmer, "the Cherokees have lost all that was valuable in their Indian character, have become spiritless, dependent and depraved." Why should Wirt waste his talents on the defense of such people? Be that as it may, Wirt's suggestion to "make up a law case" for submission to the Supreme Court was out of the question. Even if Georgia agreed to such a thing, said Gilmer, the Supreme Court had no constitutional authority to rule on a sovereign state's actions within its own borders.[16] Gilmer knew full well, however, that the purpose of such a case would be to determine where Georgia's border actually was in relation to the Cherokee Nation, an issue over which the Supreme Court's authority was without question. Nonetheless, Wirt and the Cherokees were forced to look elsewhere for a case which would bring their grievances to the Supreme Court.

The opportunity came that autumn when a Cherokee named Corn Tassels (also known as George Tassels) was convicted of murder and sentenced to hang by Judge Augustin Clayton of the Western Circuit. The case was tried in Gainesville even though, as William Underwood argued for the defense, Tassels' alleged crime was committed in the Cherokee Nation against another Cherokee. In consigning Tassels to the noose, Clayton made clear his views of Wirt and the Supreme Court: "I shall try all cases which may come under the law and wholly disregard all interference from abroad."[17] Wirt appealed to the Supreme Court for a writ of error, arguing that Georgia had no authority to try the case. On December 12, 1830, Chief Justice John Marshall cited Georgia to appear before the Court on the second Monday in January and show cause why a writ of error should not be issued. Georgia not only ignored Marshall's citation, but the General Assembly called the measure a violation of Georgia's rights and instructed all state officials, including the governor, to "disregard any and every mandate . . . from the chief justice or any associate justice of the supreme court."[18] The body also ordered that the hanging take place as soon as possible, and by the second Monday in January Corn Tassels was dead.[19]

Wirt immediately made plans for a second case to be dealt with directly by the Supreme Court. In this new appeal he asked for an injunction against the state of Georgia declaring illegal its extension of authority over the Cherokee Nation. In the spring of 1831 Indian delegations from across the country converged on Washington to lend their support in the case. David Crockett served as escort to the Cherokee representatives, introducing them to many friends in Congress who expressed sympathy for their case. Edward Everett, congressman from Massachusetts, spoke for two days on the House floor in support of the Cherokee cause. In his eloquent and moving oration, Everett lamented that Jackson and his followers had made a mockery of treaty obligations with the Indians. He suggested that these "worthless parchments," bearing the signatures of Washington, Adams, and Jefferson, be burned on the steps of the Capitol by Jackson himself. These founding fathers were gone, said Everett, "and will not witness the spectacle; but our present Chief Magistrate, as he lays them, one by one, on the fire, will see his own name subscribed on a goodly number of them. Sir, they ought to be destroyed, as a warning to the Indians to make no more compacts with us."[20] As the congressman spoke, one observer thought he heard something like a drop of rain fall upon his cloak near his ear. When the man turned and looked up, he found two Cherokees standing behind his seat. He later remembered that "the head of one of these Cherokees had fallen upon his hand, and he was endeavoring to conceal his tears."[21]

On March 12 and 14, 1831, Wirt presented his arguments before the Supreme Court in the case of *Cherokee Nation* v. *Georgia.* Attorneys for Georgia were not present since the state refused to recognize the Court's authority in the case. Wirt spoke at length on the injustices endured not only by the Cherokees but by all aboriginal Americans at the hands of their Great White Father. The Cherokee Nation, said Wirt, was a foreign nation, sovereign in its authority and secure within its borders. Neither the state of Georgia nor the federal government had a legal right to usurp Cherokee lands without Cherokee consent. However, Chief Justice Marshall's reading of the Court's decision revealed that Wirt, in preparing his argument, had made an important legal blunder. While the Court's sympathy lay with the Cherokees, they had brought suit as a foreign government. The Cherokees, said Marshall, were not a foreign nation but "a domestic, dependent nation." Since the suit was filed under this false assumption, the Court could not rule on the case.[22] Implied in this decision, however, was the Court's view that as a "dependent nation," separate and distinct from Georgia, the Cherokees might have won the case had it not been for Wirt's technical error. If the Supreme Court consistently held to its "dependent nation" view, then the state of Georgia could not have legal sanction for its extension of authority over the Cherokees. With the legal status of the Cherokee Nation now settled so far as the Supreme Court was concerned, Wirt once more sought a way to bring the issue of Georgia's actions before the Court.

The Cherokees' final opportunity for justice came in the unlikely form of a quiet, unassuming young missionary named Samuel A. Worcester. The circumstances which led to his pivotal role were put in place two years earlier, in 1830, when Georgia engulfed the Cherokee Nation. In addition to forbidding gold hunting on state lands, Georgia had also made it illegal for any white person to reside in the Cherokee country without first taking an oath to uphold the laws of the state.[23] This act was aimed primarily at the missionaries living among the Cherokees. These people were fiercely opposed to Georgia's actions and nearly as determined in their resistance to the state as the Cherokees themselves. Only a week after the creation of the Georgia Guard in December of 1830, missionaries representing the Moravians, Congregationalists, Baptists, and Presbyterians met at New Echota, the Cherokee capital, and signed a resolution supporting the Cherokee cause. The Methodists had already adopted a similar resolution.[24]

The inevitable showdown between Georgia and the missionaries came in March 1831 when the Georgia Guard arrested several churchmen, including Worcester, who refused to pledge an oath to the state. It was soon discovered, however, that these missionaries served as United States postmasters at their respective stations and as such were agents of the federal government. Section seven of the 1830 act expressly stated that the requirement to take an oath of loyalty to Georgia did not "extend to any authorized agent or agents, of the government of the United States."[25] Georgia was forced to release its captives. Though it meant freedom for the missionaries, this minor victory was all too brief. Governor Gilmer quickly wrote to Jackson asking whether he considered them government agents. The president answered that he did not, and without further inquiry had the missionaries removed from their postmaster positions.[26] Georgia was now free to move against them. A second round of arrests was made and eleven missionaries were taken into custody.

At their trial in Lawrenceville on September 15, 1831, Judge Clayton sentenced the eleven to four years at hard labor. Determined to see the missionaries recant their defiance of Georgia, Gilmer offered them executive pardon in exchange for agreeing to his terms—take the oath of loyalty to Georgia or leave the state. All but two accepted the governor's proposal. Only Samuel Worcester and Dr. Elizur Butler remained firm. The two men were promptly deposited in the state penitentiary at Milledgeville to begin their four years of laborious confinement. Even Georgians who supported the state's acquisition of Cherokee lands were appalled by this heavy-handed treatment of the missionaries. Their only recourse was an appeal to the United States Supreme Court. Here was the chance that Wirt and the Cherokees had been waiting for.

In the case of *Worcester* v. *Georgia*, Wirt based his arguments upon the Court's previous ruling that the Cherokee tribe was a dependent nation, separate and distinct from Georgia. Wirt pointed to the Constitution's provision granting exclusive authority to the federal government in matters dealing with the Indians. Treaties made with the Cherokees were still in force, and Georgia had neither the legal nor moral right to usurp federal authority as it had done.[27]

On March 23, 1832, Chief Justice Marshall handed down the Court's decision. As the gathered crowd strained to listen, the aging chief justice explained the ruling in unambiguous terms: "The Cherokee nation, then, is a distinct community, occupying its own territory, with boundaries accurately described, in which the laws of Georgia can have no force, and which the citizens of Georgia have no right to enter, but with the assent of the Cherokees themselves. . . . The act of the state of Georgia . . . is consequently void."[28] According to the Constitution, only the U.S. Government could legislate for Indians, and any state attempting to do so was in error. Worcester and the Cherokees had won.

With the status of the Cherokees legally settled, Associate Justice John McLean encouraged the Cherokee Nation to apply for statehood in order to avoid similar difficulties in the future.[29] One newspaper even suggested that the Cherokee Nation turn the tables and extend *its* authority over Georgia. "The Indians will find plenty of backers . . . in a project of this sort," said the editorial.[30] Two days after announcing the Court's ruling, Marshall issued a formal mandate ordering Georgia to release Worcester and Butler.

Chief John Ross, John Ridge, and the rest of the Cherokee Nation received the news with overwhelming joy and excitement. Under the Constitution their ancestral homeland was theirs once again. Elias Boudinot, editor of the *Cherokee Phoenix*, proclaimed the decision "a great triumph on the part of the Cherokees so far as the question of their rights [is] concerned. The question is for ever settled as to who is right and who is wrong. . . . "[31]

The Cherokees' joy was short-lived, however, for it quickly became clear that Wilson Lumpkin, the new governor of Georgia, had no intention of abiding by the Court's decision. The missionaries remained in the state penitentiary, and the Georgia Guard continued to roam the gold region enforcing the governor's will. Infuriated by this blatant disregard for the judicial process, the Cherokees sent a delegation to Washington in a last-ditch effort to obtain President Jackson's support. But there was little chance they would receive help from someone who upon hearing of the Supreme Court's decision said, "John Marshall has made his decision, now let him enforce it."[32] A meeting was arranged with the chief executive in which John Ridge, leader of the delegation, asked Jackson whether he intended to carry out his Constitutional obligation to enforce the Supreme Court's decision. Jackson replied pointedly that he had no such intention. Instead he advised Ridge to return home and tell his people that their only hope for survival as a nation was to surrender their homeland and move beyond the Mississippi.[33]

Now that the Cherokees were abandoned to the will of Georgia, hope for them seemed all but lost. They seriously considered an attempt to reintroduce their cause to the Supreme Court in a new case, but Justice McLean informally admitted to them that the Court was powerless in the face of Jackson's refusal to act against Georgia.[34] The futility of further resistance seemed evident, and Worcester and Butler wrote to Governor Lumpkin informing him that they would not press the case.[35] With Georgia's victory secure and nothing to be gained by their continued imprisonment, Lumpkin ordered the missionaries released. They had spent one year and four months as "guests" of the state penitentiary.[36]

Gloom descended not only on the Cherokees but upon the entire community of Southern Indians. They all knew that the Cherokees' failure was theirs as well. In every tribe, councils were held to discuss the impact of Georgia's extension of authority over the Cherokees and how they might combat such efforts. But the mood of these council meetings was much more depressed than it had been only weeks before. Some natives now argued that in order to preserve their nations, a move to the West was inevitable. Others urged a continuation of the struggle for their ancestral lands. The resulting factionalism, setting brother against brother, tore the Cherokee Nation apart.

Though Jackson's refusal to act was a blatant demonstration of his contempt not only for the Cherokees but for all Native Americans, it came as no surprise to those who had years of experience in dealing with the white man's government. In reflecting on a century of European encroachment, an elderly man named Speckled Snake, "whose head was whitened with the frost of more than a hundred winters," put it this way in an address to his fellow Indians:

> Brothers! I have listened to many talks from our great father. When he first came over the wide waters, he was but a little man . . . very little. His legs were cramped by sitting long in his big boat, and he begged for a little land to light his fire on. . . . But when the white man had warmed himself before the Indians' fire and filled himself with their hominy, he became very large. With a

step he bestrode the mountains, and his feet covered the plains and the valleys. His hands grasped the eastern and the western sea, and his head rested on the moon. Then he became our Great Father. He loved his red children, and he said, "Get a little further, lest I tread on thee."

Brothers! I have listened to a great many talks from our great father. But they always began and ended in this—"Get a little further; you are too near me."[37]

Native Americans were not the only ones to recognize the injustice they had suffered or to feel the frustration of resistance to the tide now overtaking them. Many white friends expressed similar disgust at the evident greed of the intruders. For his part Judge William Underwood continued to argue on behalf of the Cherokees at every opportunity. On one occasion he visited a Baptist preacher near Gainesville whom he knew to be an honest and just man. This preacher was very influential in the community, and Underwood felt that he might be of some help to the Cherokee cause. In their conversation Underwood reviewed the long history of Anglo injustice inflicted on the natives. From the initial atrocities of colonial times to Georgia's present attempt to expel the Cherokees, he told of the misery suffered by Native Americans at the hands of Europeans and their descendants. "And now," said the Judge in conclusion, "Parson, is not our State doing a grievous wrong, for which God will hold us and our children to fearful accounts?"

"Yes, Judge," replied the reverend, "it looks very much as you say."

"Looks!" shouted Underwood, "Looks!!" "But is it not so?"

"Yes!" responded the preacher. "I *reckon* it is as you say. But then, Judge," said this honest man of God, "we want the land!"

Judge Underwood could only shake his head in reply and lament, "Yes, we want the land! Good God Almighty!"[38]

Chapter Four

"Civilized Life"
Comes to the Gold Region

With a promise of noninterference from Jackson, Georgia was left a free hand in what was now solidly its northern territory. On the first Monday of February 1831, elections were held across the state for ninety-six district surveyors. Each county selected at least one surveyor, and the twenty most populous counties were granted two. Later that year these men headed north and began partitioning the Cherokee lands.[1] Teams consisting of a surveyor, a chain carrier, a pack carrier, two axe men, and a cook roamed the hills and valleys of north Georgia for months preparing the region to be raffled off in a statewide lottery scheduled to begin in the autumn of 1832. The General Assembly instructed survey teams "to mark, or cause to be marked, plainly and distinctly, upon trees, if practicable, otherwise on posts, all stations and all lines which may be required to run." They divided the territory into four 27-mile-wide sections, each containing a designated number of nine-square-mile districts.[2]

It was also the surveyors' task to designate those districts in which gold had been found. The Gold Districts, of which there were thirty-three, were divided into lots of 40 acres each, while the Land Districts, numbering sixty, were divided into lots of 160 acres. Those lands on the edge of the survey area that could not be laid off into complete 160- or 40-acre lots were called fractional lots.[3]

The practice of distributing land by lottery was unique to Georgia. Dating back to 1805 when the first lottery was held, this method was developed in the wake of the Yazoo land fraud of 1795. A storm of protest erupted when it was discovered that state officials had taken bribes from speculators in exchange for special favors in purchasing large tracts of land in what would later become Alabama and Mississippi. Reaction to the scandal was so fierce that the state agreed to give up land claims between the Chattahoochee and Mississippi rivers and to develop a less offensive means of land distribution.

Under the new lottery system, stolen Indian lands were incorporated into adjacent Georgia counties and surveyed into land lots. Citizens of the state, but not the native Indians, could then register for a lottery in which these lands would be raffled off. Each qualified citizen was entitled to at least one chance. Persons belonging to specially designated groups, such as veterans, orphans, or heads of families, were given two chances. Tickets bearing the names of the registrants were sent to the state capital at Milledgeville, where they were placed in a large rotating drum. Tickets with land lot numbers written on them were deposited in a second drum. Both drums were spun simultaneously, and one ticket was drawn from each. On payment of a nominal fee, the person whose name was drawn became the owner of the land lot shown on the matched ticket.[4] Between 1805 and 1827, five lotteries were held to parcel out Indian lands. The lottery of 1832, the sixth and final one, would expel the Cherokees.

Though most Georgians were intrigued by the prospect of a lottery in which they might actually win a gold mine, there was nonetheless considerable opposition to the idea. Many believed it a terrible waste to distribute the state's wealth in such a haphazard fashion. In a vein of classical socialism, Governor Gilmer himself argued that it would be more beneficial for the state to operate the mines. Gilmer was no friend of the Cherokees, but he did believe that through state operation of the gold mines, taxes could be lowered, improvements on roads and navigable rivers could be made, and revenues could be generated for public education. Said Gilmer, "Mines . . . should be managed for the general and not the individual advantage."[5]

Besides his concern for the public welfare, Gilmer worried that a lottery involving gold mines might lead to rampant land speculation—the very thing that the lottery was originally designed to avoid. Prophetically, he predicted that the rapid buying and selling of gold lands would result in frauds committed against both the state and individual land owners. Furthermore, Gilmer feared that "regular industry and economy might be suspended by . . . imaginary gains" if Georgians were encouraged by a gold lottery to "hope of acquiring great wealth without labor."[6] Gilmer seems to have been unaware that a great deal of labor is involved in any type of mining, but as it turned out, he was right about the runaway speculation and resulting frauds.

The lottery issue was hotly debated in the gubernatorial campaign of 1831. Wilson Lumpkin, Gilmer's opponent, made no

Benjamin Parks, one of the first to discover gold in Georgia. Though he mined for years, he never struck it rich. As an old man in his nineties, "Uncle Benny" said of gold mining, "It's just like gambling—all luck." Georgia Department of Archives and History.

GOLD.--A gentleman of the first respectability in Habersham county, writes us thus, under date of 22d July :

"Two gold mines have just been discovered in this county, and preparations are making to bring these hidden treasures of the earth into use."

So it appears that what we long anticipated has come to pass at last, namely, that the gold region of North and South Carolina, would be found to extend into Georgia. And another anticipation of ours will hereafter come to pass, namely, that it will be a sad day for Georgia, when the precious metals are found in any great abundance in her soil. The best thing that the Legislature could do, would be to prohibit under severe penalties, the working of any gold or silver mines in the State. Those who live to see the result will be convinced to their sorrow that this advice is not founded on a slight or partial consideration of the subject.

Despite numerous "first discovery" claims, the first evidence of a gold strike in Georgia was this brief notice which appeared in a Milledgeville newspaper, the *Georgia Journal*, on August 1, 1829.

In an interview that appeared in the *Atlanta Constitution* on July 15, 1894, Benjamin Parks recalled the first days of the gold rush. "The news got abroad, and such excitement you never saw. . . . All the way from where Dahlonega now stands to Nuckollsville [Auraria] there were men panning out of the branches and making holes in the hillsides." From "Gold Mining in Georgia," *Harper's*, 1879.

John Ross, principal chief of the Cherokee Nation. Ross fought against removal to the end and lost his wife, Quatie, on the Trail of Tears. Georgia Department of Archives and History.

Major Ridge, leader of the Cherokee faction that favored a removal treaty. Though initially opposed to removal, he later came to feel that it was the only way to ensure the Cherokees' survival as a nation. Smithsonian Institution, National Anthropological Archives.

David Crockett of Tennessee, one of the few Southern congressmen who opposed the Indian Removal Act of 1830. He knew his position was political suicide, but insisted, "I would sooner be honestly and politically d——nd, than hypocritically immortalized." Painting by Pierre Saint Jean, 1828.

Andrew Jackson, or, as this 1832 campaign caricature called him, "King Andrew the First." In his left hand he holds his favorite legislative tool, the veto, and under his feet are the shredded remains of, among other documents, the United States Constitution. Library of Congress.

George Gilmer, governor of Georgia (1829–31, 1837–39), opposed the distribution of gold lands by the lottery system. He argued that the state ought to control the mines, saying that they "should be managed for the general and not the individual advantage." Georgia Department of Archives and History.

Wilson Lumpkin, governor of Georgia (1831–35), supported the lottery. By election day the voters of Georgia were, as the *Cherokee Phoenix* put it, "sick with the expectation of Indian land and gold," and Lumpkin became the new governor. Georgia Department of Archives and History.

Land Lottery Drawing. Developed in the wake of the Yazoo land fraud, Georgia's land lottery system was the only one of its kind in the United States. In 1832–33 the Cherokee Nation was, as one contemporary put it, gambled away in Georgia's sixth and final land lottery. Sketch by George I. Parrish, Jr. Georgia Department of Archives and History.

Panning for gold. This was the simplest and most widely used method during the early days of the gold rush. Even using more elaborate methods, miners were usually fortunate to pan out five dollars a day. The average was less than half that amount. In this 1934 photo, a poor farmer supplements his income by panning along the banks of Long Branch, five miles south of Dahlonega. Georgia Department of Archives and History.

The cradle rocker was one of the most widely used placer mining devices in the Southern gold fields. Gold-bearing dirt was washed through a perforated plate, or "hopper," and riffle bars trapped small particles of gold in the lower trough. University of North Carolina Library.

Another popular device of the 1830s was the sluice box, widely used for more than a century. In this 1912 image, Bill and Tom Jenkins use a sluice box to hunt for gold on Tanyard Branch in Tate's Pasture, now part of North Georgia College. Georgia Department of Archives and History.

The "hollow gum" rocker. A continuous flow of water washed rich sand and gravel over riffle bars, which trapped the heavy gold particles. One miner "rocked" the device while the other shoveled in dirt and agitated it with a rake. From Phillips, "Essay on the Georgia Gold Mines," 1833.

This type of sluice box allowed particles of gold to pass through holes in an iron plate to be trapped in an inclined box below. From Phillips, "Essay on the Georgia Gold Mines," 1833.

This contraption, mounted on rollers, combined the action of the gum rocker and the sluice box but channeled the water into an upper perforated trough. This method reduced the danger of gold being washed out and lost by the direct force of flowing water. From Phillips, "Essay on the Georgia Gold Mines," 1833.

1832 LOTTERY DISTRICTS

Section 1

| 18 | 17 | 9 | 8 |
| 19 | 16 | 10 | 7 |

Chestatee River

Chattahoochee River

Section 2

8	9	27	10	9	28	9	10
7	10	26	11	8	27	8	11
6	11	25	12	7	26	7	12
5	12	24	13	6	25	6	13
4	13	23	14	5	24	5	14

Section 3

Section 4

ALABAMA

Gold Districts

1832 Lottery Districts

promise of lower taxes but enthusiastically supported the lottery. Lumpkin cited as evidence for his position what he contemptuously referred to as the need for "a settled freehold population on every part of our territory . . . hitherto the abode of a people wholly unqualified to enjoy the blessings of wise self-government."[7] Newspapers across the state took up the argument. Some editorial comments, like this one in the *Macon Advertiser*, strongly supported Gilmer: "The Question At Issue—The two propositions which now present themselves for the decision of Georgia are: Gilmer and the Laws and Lumpkin and Taxation!!! Will the people hesitate which of the two to choose? They cannot, they will not. Let their cry be on the first Monday in October, Long Life to Gilmer! Long Life to the Laws! And Down, Down with Lumpkin and His Abominable System of Taxation!!!"[8] However, another Macon paper more accurately represented the general feeling among Georgia voters toward Gilmer's plan to "reserve" the mines with this editorial. "Reservation of the Gold Mines—As it relates to the poorer portion of our population, the injustice of Governor Gilmer's policy in regard to this subject has been ably stated and demonstrated. It is believed that not one voice in five hundred is raised in favor of his recommendation."[9]

By election time the voters of Georgia were, as the *Cherokee Phoenix* put it, "sick with the expectation of Indian land and gold." It was obvious that no candidate could be elected without supporting the lottery. One disturbed Cherokee wrote of Georgia's electorate, "This class is numerous, and all ignorant—they do not know anything about writs of error, the constitution of the United States, etc. They know they are poor and wish to be rich, and believe that, if they have luck, they will draw a gold mine, and most everyone expects to have his luck in the lottery."[10] With the additional attractions of such estates as those of John Ridge, John Ross, and David Vann, it is hardly surprising that ethical questions involving the lottery were given scant attention. George Paschal, whose family had eleven chances in the lottery, displayed unusual candor when he wrote, "the immorality, if any were admitted . . . was so infinitesimally divided among seven hundred thousand people, that no one felt the crushing weight of responsibility."[11] A popular ditty of the time summed up the general attitude.[12]

> All I want in this creation
> Is a pretty little wife and a big plantation
> Away up yonder in the Cherokee nation

The temptation proved too great for Georgians to overcome. On October 3, 1831, they sold their votes for the promise of Cherokee land and gold, and Wilson Lumpkin became the new governor.

Still there were many Georgians, residents of the gold region among them, who deeply regretted what they viewed as the waste of a valuable natural resource. They agreed with Gilmer and felt that the mines might have provided employment for thousands and forever done away with the need for taxation. Wrote one disappointed citizen, "It is indeed painful for one who feels as a Georgian should, to contrast Georgia as she is, with Georgia as she might have been."[13] But such objections were made in vain. Lumpkin's day was here and lottery's would soon follow.

In the act authorizing a lottery, the General Assembly designated those persons qualified to participate and determined the number of chances to which each was entitled. For the 160-acre land lots, qualified individuals were defined as "every male white person of eighteen years of age . . . and an inhabitant . . . of this state, four years. Every deaf and dumb or blind person of like residence. . . . All widows. . . . All families of orphans." Heads of families, "families of orphans consisting of more than two," veterans of the wars with Great Britain or the Indians, and widows or orphans of such veterans were entitled to additional chances.[14] Qualifications for the 40-acre gold lots were generally the same, except that one need have been a resident of the state for only three years instead of four.[15]

The General Assembly was also specific with regard to those who could not register for the drawing. Any person who had taken out a grant on land won in a previous lottery was barred. Convicted felons and those who were or had been associated with "a certain horde of thieves known as the Pony Club" were excluded from participation in the lottery. And, of course, the Cherokees were excluded by Section 16 of the Lottery Act which forbade participation by any resident of the Cherokee Nation.[16]

Section 15 of the act excluded those who had mined gold in the area since June 1, 1830, when the practice was made illegal. This provision, which was originally included by an opponent of the bill hoping thus to ensure its defeat, met with a storm of protest from the counties bordering Cherokee lands. Many of their residents had crossed into the forbidden territory after the cutoff date and mined for gold. One local man suggested that the upper counties call a convention to nullify the act or else secede from the lower counties of Georgia. "Of what worth to us is continuance of this union with them," asked the irate miner, "when it is used to divest us of the rights of freedom?" In reality few miners were excluded by this provision. Such a violation was difficult to prove unless one were caught in the process. Section 15 was not nullified, and the Lottery Act remained unchanged.[17]

By September 1832 the surveys were complete, and all across the state people flocked to their respective county seats to register for the drawing. The names were sent to the state capital at Milledgeville, where they were deposited in the huge lottery drums.[18] These drums were constructed at the state penitentiary during the confinement of Samuel Worcester and Elizur Butler, and there was a rumor that the two missionaries had been forced against their will to help build them. In an open letter, Worcester and Butler dispelled this rumor and commended the warden for his sensitivity to their feelings in the matter.[19]

On October 22, 1832, the state of Georgia, as one lottery opponent put it, began gambling away its rich inheritance.[20] The twin drums were spun and names and tickets were drawn by the thousands. According to one account, the wooden drums were so heavy when filled with tickets that even a strong man could hardly turn them.[21] To conduct the lottery, the General Assembly provided for the employment of commissioners, clerks, ticket drawers, and a doorkeeper.[22]

In the land lottery there were 85,000 people competing for 18,309 prizes. Blank tickets were placed in the prize drum to bring their number up to that of the number of registrants. These odds meant that about three out of every four hopeful participants won nothing but a worthless slip of paper. In the gold lottery there were 133,000 names registered to draw for 35,000 lots. Again, as in the land lottery, about three out of four people came away empty-handed.[23] For a "fortunate drawer" to claim a prize, he or she took an oath testifying to qualification and paid an eighteen-dollar grant fee. If the winner of a lot did not take out a grant, the land became state property.[24]

Even before the lottery began, gold mining companies were set up with the intention of purchasing gold lots as they were drawn. By 1832 the location of the best mining sites was common knowledge, and many of the new mining companies had already selected the lots they planned to purchase. One such enterprise was formed by five men in Jefferson, Georgia, and called, appropriately, the Jefferson Mining Company. The Pigeon Roost lot, just across the Chestatee River in Cherokee territory, was known to be one of the richest of the gold lots, and it was to this spot that the Jefferson Company directed its attention. Allen Matthews, the company's president, and a Mr. Appleby, its secretary and treasurer, moved to Nuckollsville, later named Auraria, when the lottery got under way. The two men were authorized to pay as much as ten thousand dollars for the lot when the opportunity presented itself. They employed a man named Higginbottom to go to Milledgeville and, when the Pigeon Roost lot was drawn, to locate the winner and bring him to Nuckollsville.

The Jefferson Company was not the only corporation interested in Pigeon Roost, but as it happened the lot was drawn late one evening after most spectators were gone. Despite the hour Higginbottom set out to find the new owner of Pigeon Roost, who lived 130 miles south of Milledgeville. By the time the evening's drawing was posted the next morning, Higginbottom had a fifty-mile head start.

The fortunate winner of the drawing turned out to be a poor farmer who worked land owned by a Colonel Hampton. Higginbottom had a difficult time convincing the man that he was the new owner of a gold mine, and the man could not read the instructions from the Jefferson Company that Higginbottom had with him. They went to see Hampton, who confirmed the story. "You go with this man," Hampton told his tenant. "Allen Matthews is an old friend of mine. . . . You can rely on him." Hampton penned a letter to Matthews explaining that the winner of the drawing was a poor man and that no advantage should be taken of him. Next morning Higginbottom and the tenant farmer started for the gold region.

When they arrived at Nuckollsville, Matthews advised the man to announce that on a certain day he would take sealed bids on the lot. The highest bidder would receive the deed. The farmer repeatedly asked if he might expect to get as much as a thousand dollars for his lot, and Matthews answered, perhaps with a wry grin, "I guess you can." On the appointed day a large crowd gathered at the Matthews home in Jefferson to witness the bidding. Dr. Hull, a local physician, was chosen from among the spectators to open the bids. A pile of envelopes was placed on a table in the front yard, and the nervous farmer sat on the porch as Dr. Hull read the bids aloud. They ranged from two thousand to eight thousand dollars, except for the bid of the Jefferson Company, which was ten thousand. The formerly poor seller was beside himself with joy. Here was more money than he had hoped to see in a lifetime. With this new-found wealth the man purchased his own farm in south Georgia and saw that his children received a good education. The Jefferson Company worked its lot for about a year before it sold out and was renamed by its new owners the Pigeon Roost Mining Company.[25]

Other fortunate lottery winners received similarly impressive offers for their lots, but some decided to work their mines themselves. One such person was Mary G. Franklin, a poor widow who lived in Clarke County near Athens. Not long after the lottery began, she was informed that the drums had favored her with a 40-acre gold lot located about five miles southeast of Ball Ground on the Etowah River in what is today Cherokee County. Within a week of winning the lot, she received at least a dozen offers. Desiring to see this gold mine for herself, the old woman mounted her gray mule and headed north. Upon her arrival she found twenty miners at work panning out gold on the lot. She quickly found a trustworthy man to help her drive off the intruders and placed him in charge of the property until she could return with her family. Fortune favored the old woman with a rich piece of land, and the enterprise that she established turned out to be so productive that Mrs. Franklin eventually bought the adjoining lots and expanded her business into one of the largest gold mining operations in Georgia.[26]

By far the two most sought after of the gold lots were located just east of Dahlonega on Yahoola Creek.[27] These adjacent lots, numbered 1031 and 1052, were long known to contain rich gold deposits. It was to this spot in particular that men would sneak across the Chestatee River at night and carry off old meal bags full of dirt to be panned out on safer ground.[28] Anxious crowds watched the spinning drums day after day to see who the lucky winners of these lots would be, but neither was drawn until the last week of the lottery. Among the most excited spectators was a man by the name of Mosely who made up his mind to win lot 1052 or purchase it from the fortunate winner if he could. After six months of waiting, he finally heard lottery officials call out, "Section 1, district 2, number 1052—Alford Allison." Mosely immediately set out for Greene County, the address given for the Allison residence, twenty miles northeast of Milledgeville. He found the poor farmer behind a plow and asked if he might be willing to sell. When Allison recovered from the initial shock of hearing of his good fortune, he told Mosely that he was not sure if he wanted to sell his lot. After repeated offers Allison finally relented, but the purchase almost bankrupted Mosely. What little money he had left went into equipment for his new mine. Though the site held a reputation for being rich in gold, Mosely spent several fruitless years working the lot. The unfortunate man could never make a profit from his efforts and was finally forced to sell the mine for a fraction of his original investment. Soon after this change of hands, a rich vein was discovered on the property, and the mine produced a wealth of gold for its new owner, the original lottery winner, Alford Allison.[29]

Though a great many people made fortunes by selling their lots, and at least one in buying his back, attempts by mining companies to cheat the lucky out of their winnings were common. Each drawing of a gold lot initiated a race among these companies to find the fortunate winner and purchase the land. The first company representative to locate a winner would try by any means to obtain the lot at the lowest possible cost. The next to arrive would reveal to the winner that he had been cheated out of a fortune. Meanwhile, the first company hurried to the mine and took out as much gold as possible before the appearance of agents from the second company, with the winner in tow. The late arrivals would employ lawyers to swear out injunctions to restrain the first company until ownership of the land could be settled.[30] In most cases the lot's value did not warrant such efforts by either company. With so many of these suits being taken out, it was usually the lawyers who "made off with a gold mine."

With so much land to be won in the lottery, it was almost inevitable that the system would be plagued with fraud of every type. The most prevalent illegalities involved unqualified persons who registered for the drawing. Some people registered even though they were citizens neither of Georgia nor of the United States. Others had not been residents of the state for the requisite three years for gold lots or four for land lots. In some cases people claimed to be orphans when in fact their parents were very much alive. In one instance a man from Tattnall County named Allen Summerall registered for a chance in the lottery as a single white male. Only later did the authorities discover that his mother was of African-American descent. According to Georgia law, this made Summerall a "free person of color" and as such ineligible for the drawing.[31]

To give citizens an incentive to report those who participated in the lottery illegally, the General Assembly stipulated that any person who provided information necessary to prosecute the fraudulent lottery participant would receive a portion, usually half, of the lot in question. The other half became state property. This system proved cumbersome since a division of the lot satisfactory to both parties was difficult to negotiate. To offer an alternative means of settlement, the Assembly passed an act stating that if the informant gave his consent, the lot could be sold and the proceeds divided equally between the state and the informant.[32]

Fraud was by no means confined to the general populace. Occasionally the lottery officials themselves were found to lack integrity. One such official was Shadrach Bogan of Lawrenceville, a commissioner of the land lottery, who was impeached in late 1832 for "high crimes, misdemeanor, and forgery." It seems that Bogan had arranged to draw certain tracts of land for himself, among them the residence of Major Ridge. The property was worth an estimated forty thousand dollars.[33]

By May 1833 the lottery was completed, and thousands of "fortunate drawers," as they were called, flooded into the gold region seeking out their newly acquired lands. But these people were forbidden by the state to occupy their lots if native Cherokees lived on them. According to Georgia law, they were to wait until the Cherokees either moved voluntarily or were forced by the state to do so. For a lottery winner to attempt to coerce a Cherokee off his land meant forfeiture of the prize. Even if the Cherokees agreed to vacate, they were to be paid for improvements such as houses, barns, wells, and fences that they had made on the property.[34] To enforce those Cherokee property rights that the Assembly grudgingly admitted, Georgia authorized the creation of an inadequate eleven-man force to patrol the area and expel intruders.[35] Even this small compensation was negated in 1834 by the passage of an act allowing gold and land lot winners to "test the same for gold and operate thereon" regardless of Cherokee occupancy.[36]

Legislation protecting Cherokee property rights was worth little more than the paper it was written on. No sooner were the winners told of their good fortune than they rushed to take possession of their prizes without compensation to the previous occupants. So anxious were some lucky drawers to see their newly won lands that they began arriving only a few weeks after the lottery started. A November 24, 1832, editorial in the *Cherokee Phoenix* complained that "the fortunate drawers (so called) *of our lands* have been passing and repassing single and in companies . . . in search of the splendid lots which the rolling wheel has pictured to their imaginations. 'Ho, sir! Where is the nearest line to this place, what district, number, corner, lot, station, etc.' are the impertinent questions forced upon us." The writer pointed out that the Cherokees had not relinquished title to the land and were under no obligation to do so. "We hold," he wrote, "the bond and seal of the republic to protect this property." He reminded his readers that the Cherokee Nation had given up vast tracts of land to the United States in exchange for that protection. Furthermore, the Indian Removal Act of 1830 provided that existing treaties would not be violated, and the Supreme Court had declared Georgia's encroachment illegal. Even the courts of Georgia upheld the property rights of individual Cherokee landowners. The writer concluded with these words: "Let us, therefore, calmly wait and see if the government will not yet acquiesce to the numerous authorities we have cited, from which we claim our relief; or whether the government will choose to have [its] laws nullified by a state as the easiest mode of releasing itself from enforcing them."[37] They did not have to wait long. President Jackson continued to ignore the issue, and Georgia quickly proceeded to occupy its claim.

The gold rush and subsequent lottery drew thousands of people to Georgia. Such a rapid influx of miners and adventurers resulted in a dramatic increase in trade and commerce. This brought wealth to those towns on the edge of Cherokee country and led to the establishment of gold rush boom towns. As an editor of the *Macon Advertiser* put it, "The rapid advance and improvement in the northern and western part of the State has already given to those sections of the country an interest and attention with which it was thought, four years ago, they would never be invested. Numerous flourishing villages have sprung up there as if by magic, and their enterprising settlers are pursuing all the diversified avocations of civilized life."[38]

Georgia's entire Cherokee acquisition was designated Cherokee County in December 1831 for administrative purposes and to prepare the region for distribution by lottery. On the first Monday in February 1832, those persons "entitled to vote for members of the General Assembly"[39] met at the home of Ambrose Harnage and held the county's first elections. At the time there were about 130 white families living in the Cherokee region, 67 of which lived within ten miles of the Harnage place.[40] Under the supervision of three justices of the peace, they set up an Inferior Court and elected a sheriff, a tax collector, a coroner, and other county officials. The county was made part of the Western Judicial

Circuit, and in March 1832 the first session of the Superior Court was held at the Harnage house.

This frontier village was a stagecoach stop and post office on the Federal Road that ran from Tennessee through the Cherokee Nation and into Georgia. The settlement was called Harnageville in the act creating Cherokee County. Ambrose Harnage was a squatter who held no title to the land, and it was drawn in the lottery by "a man named Fawns" from Savannah. The Harnage property was purchased two years later by Samuel Tate, who opened a hotel and tavern. Since then the town has been known as Tate.[41]

At the next session of the General Assembly in December 1832, the area was further divided into the counties of Union, Murray, Paulding, Forsyth, Gilmer, Cobb, Floyd, Lumpkin, Cherokee, and Cass.[42] Though by law the region was closed to intrusion until the lottery's end, white settlements began to spring up in the Cherokee country long before the lottery drawings even started. This was particularly true in the richest part of the gold region in Lumpkin County, parts of which are today White and Dawson Counties.

The first of the gold rush boom towns was six miles south of where Dahlonega now stands. In June 1832 William Dean built a cabin here on a ridge between the Chestatee and Etowah rivers.[43] At this point the two rivers are only a couple of miles apart, but they never meet. The Etowah's waters flow westward, eventually forming part of the Mobile River, which enters the Gulf of Mexico at Mobile Bay. The Chestatee winds its way to the south, joining with the Chattahoochee, which eventually flows into the Apalachicola River and enters the Gulf at Apalachicola, Florida.

When Lumpkin County was organized in 1832, its temporary seat was called simply "the place where William Dean now lives."[44] Shortly after Dean built his cabin, Nathaniel Nuckolls arrived in the area and built a small tavern and hotel along with several log and frame buildings to house the miners. His establishment was so popular that the town quickly expanded and came to be called Nuckollsville, sometimes spelled Knucklesville. The latter spelling was usually a simple mistake, but many people said that it was a reflection of frequent brawls that took place between the rough-and-tumble miners.[45]

The population of Nuckollsville grew rapidly, especially after the lottery began in October 1832. Within six months the town contained "one hundred family dwellings, eighteen or twenty stores, twelve or fifteen law offices, and four or five taverns."[46] One

Macon newspaper called this development "unprecedented in any back country village of the Southern states."[47] By May 1833 the town's population was around 1,000, and there were an estimated 10,000 people in the county.[48] The self-proclaimed town poet, who went by the name of Billy, wrote of its burgeoning populace:

> And as for people, they're so thick,
> That you might stir them with a stick;
> And every house you see will *grin*
> To show you what may be within.
> Of people, we've of every hue,
> Some white, red, yaller, *black and blue:*
> Others with dirt, so covered well,
> What color they, I could not tell.[49]

As the town grew, its people became increasingly dissatisfied with the "Knucklesville" designation, and several alternatives were suggested. Some joked that it might appropriately be called "Scuffle-town" or "Chuckluck City" as a reflection of its character. Senator John C. Calhoun of South Carolina, who owned a local mine and was a frequent visitor, also expressed an interest in having the town renamed. In November 1832 a traveling companion of Calhoun, one Dr. Croft, suggested *Aureola*, meaning "golden," as a name for this gold rush settlement. He also suggested *Aldoradda*, a derivative of the Spanish *El Dorado*, or "gold region," as an appropriate name for the county.[50] Calhoun liked both names and urged adoption of one or the other, but the citizens finally settled on *Auraria*, from the Latin *aurum*, meaning "gold." The name was suggested by a local citizen named John Powell, though the honor has sometimes mistakenly been attributed to Calhoun.[51] The notion that the name Auraria originated with Calhoun seems to have come from an article entitled "The Georgia Gold Region" that appeared in *Niles' Register* on May 4, 1833. Quoting a correspondence from Charleston, South Carolina, the article states that the name "was adopted on the suggestion of Mr. Calhoun." Based on this erroneous article, Andrew Cain in his *History of Lumpkin County* also attributed the naming of Auraria to Calhoun.[52]

Though the town now had a more respectable name, whatever its origin, old habits proved hard for some folks to break. In spite of its negative connotation, the term "Nuckollsville" was never completely abandoned. Many of the local residents continued to use it, and the old name could still be heard around Auraria well into the twentieth century.[53]

With its new name and growing population, Auraria seemed to have a bright future. The lottery was scheduled to end in May 1833, and Auraria, the only sizable town in the area and the provisional county seat, was certain to be made the official center of county government. But shortly before the Inferior Court[54] met to designate the county seat, a serious problem arose. It was learned that the 40-acre lot on which most of Auraria stood had been won in the lottery by a man named John R. Plummer of Walton County, whose right to participate in the drawing had been questioned by Nathaniel Nuckolls. Plummer registered for two chances in the lottery, claiming to be head of a household. As luck would have it, he won two gold lots, one of them in Auraria. Nuckolls then informed Judge John H. Hooper of the Cherokee Circuit that Plummer had neither a wife nor children.[55] With the need to establish a stable county government pressing and the ultimate fate of Auraria in doubt, the court had little choice but to choose a new site for the court house.[56]

Even with difficulties concerning Auraria apparent, there was considerable disagreement among the five judges. Two argued for a location about six miles to the north. A third was undecided, and a fourth insisted on Auraria despite its possible legal inconveniences. A fifth member of the court did not attend but was known to favor Auraria. Under pressure from the first two, the undecided judge voted for relocation. Had the fifth judge been present, the vote might easily have gone the other way.[57]

On April 24, 1833, the court announced its selection of a site north of Auraria near the Cane Creek mining activities. Aurarians protested loudly against losing the county seat. Some went so far as to suggest that Auraria and its immediate vicinity secede from the rest of the county. The two dissenting judges, William Dean and A. K. Blackwell, ran a statement in the *Western Herald* disavowing any acquiescence to the court's decision and promising to do everything they could to have it reversed. The site agreed upon, declared Dean and Blackwell, was "altogether ineligible, and inconvenient, being neither in a central neighborhood for the county, as it refers to place or population."[58] In June a group of Auraria's citizens called a town meeting "for the purpose of expressing their sentiments respecting the location of the Court House." Those in attendance presented various impassioned arguments against the Cane Creek site and in favor of their own town. One man cited geographical evidence demonstrating the impracticality of the new county seat, stating that the court had made its choice "either from an ignorance of the Geography of the county, or from selfish or interested motives."[59]

Auraria suffered its final indignity with its Fourth of July celebration. Isaac R. Walker, who was originally scheduled make an address at Auraria, was enticed to participate in the Independence Day festivities at the new county seat. Even Judge Blackwell, who had favored Auraria, attended the rival celebration.[60] Adding injury to insult, the new county seat announced a sale of town lots to commence on July 3 and continue through the sixth. This move to draw people to the county seat's celebration effectively killed any chance Auraria had for a large turnout at its own gathering. Nonetheless, Aurarians held their Fourth of July celebration, small though it was, and drank a toast to the new seat of Lumpkin County—"Conceived in sin, brought forth in iniquity, cradled in corruption and located upon destruction."[61]

Auraria witnessed a drastic decline during the summer of 1833. Town lots were put up for sale or abandoned, and businesses and county offices began relocating to the new seat of government. In July both the sheriff and the clerk of the Superior Court moved their offices to the new town.[62] A month later, on August 22, 1833, the first session of the Superior Court of Lumpkin County was held in a small log structure located in what is now the middle of the street just north of the Dahlonega Courthouse Gold Museum.[63]

The courthouse was situated on Lot 950, District 12, Section 1. This place had gone by several names since the beginning of the gold rush, "Head Quarters" and "New Mexico" among them. It also seems to have been called "Licklog" since this was where Lewis Ralston and Benjamin Parks put out salt for their livestock.[64] The town soon became known as Dahlonega, and it is this name that has become synonymous with the Georgia gold rush.

The name Dahlonega, from the Cherokee "dalanigei" meaning "yellow money" or gold, was indeed appropriate.[65] Gold was so abundant in the area that during the gold rush and for many years thereafter boys often collected sand that washed into the town streets after a shower and panned out small flakes of gold.[66] The town was given its name in October 1833 by the Inferior Court, and an announcement in the Western Herald gave a spelling of the town's name as "Talonega." For a while there was some confusion as to what the correct spelling should be.[67] An act of the General Assembly incorporating the town spelled its name "Talonaga."[68] A Cherokee who had "the advantages of a classical education" informed the editor of the *Western Herald* that the correct spelling should be "Dahlohnega." The editor added, "Thus, many with ourselves have been deceived by the similarity of the sound in the 'D' and 'T'—the propriety of the additional 'H' in the first and second syllables, must strike those who have been accustomed to hearing the natives pronounce this word; as it gives an idea of the Indian aspirate; separates the proper syllables, and enables the eye at once to recognize a word, before known only to the ear."[69]

Despite the learned Cherokee's advice, the spelling of Lumpkin County's new seat continued to cause confusion—a predicament that is still appreciated by modern visitors to the town. People across the state spelled it the way they thought it was pronounced, resulting in such amusing mistakes as "Tahlauneca" and "Dablobuega."[70] But by the end of 1833 the townspeople settled on the spelling "Dahlonega."

With its establishment as the county seat, Dahlonega experienced the rapid development that had earlier characterized Auraria. As the editor of the *Western Herald* put it, "The village is improving with unprecedented rapidity."[71] Almost overnight the town was divided into lots selling for between two hundred and five hundred dollars each.[72] Within a few months nearly a thousand people were crowded into the settlement with about five thousand in the surrounding hills.[73]

Other Georgia counties also profited from a concentration of gold in their soil. Northeast of and adjacent to Lumpkin were Habersham and Rabun counties, just outside the Cherokee Nation.[74] With its rich Nacoochee Valley gold district, Habersham County boasted some of the most productive mines in Georgia. Only a few years earlier, the first white settlers in the valley had been able to buy land from the Cherokees for as little as one cent an acre.[75] As it turned out, these pioneers had unknowingly made one of the best investments on record. Newspapers of the day carried almost weekly reports of incredible success at the Nacoochee mines.[76] A local man named Henry Clay bought a mine for five thousand dollars and, employing 23 workers, regained his initial investment in only nine weeks.[77] R. R. Winfrey, superintendent at the McGehee and White Mine, brought out almost a thousand dollars' worth of gold in a five-day period with 15 workers. Winfrey claimed that this represented "the largest amount of gold obtained in this or any other country in the same time and with the same number of hands."[78]

Newspaper editors across the state added their voices to the chorus of praise for the Habersham County mines. One editor went so far as to state that "the vein mines in the Naucoochy settlement are richer . . . than those in the [Cherokee] Nation" (a direct reference to Lumpkin County).[79] Said another, "Habersham can truly boast of the largest specimens of Gold which have yet been found in Georgia. . . . the Loudsville, and the McLaughlin mines, are not excelled in richness by any in the United States."[80]

Clarkesville was the boom town of this part of the Georgia gold belt. By 1831 it had eleven stores, four law offices, a confectionery shop, several machine shops, and the Jacob Stroup Iron Works. The town also had two churches, but their presence was greatly overshadowed by three taverns and a local brewery.[81] Clarkesville was, after all, a gold rush town. Even so, a visitor described the bustling mountain community in 1833 as "very pretty, with numerous well-built frame houses, and a brick court-house in the middle of its square."[82] The *Macon Advertiser* said of Clarkesville, "No village presents a better field for the exertion of the adventurers, the man of capital or business; and there is everything around it to make it one of the most fashionable summer resorts in the South."[83]

The town of Gainesville, just south of the Cherokee Nation in Hall County, also experienced a boom period during the gold rush. It was already the largest town bordering the Cherokee Nation, and it quickly became a center of trade and a gateway to the gold region. The town's businesses took in an amount of gold worth $120,000 in 1830, and the next year an expansion project laid out eight or ten new streets.[84] Hall County was also a significant gold producing area in its own right. In 1830 a man named Elrod opened "one of the richest gold mines yet discovered in Georgia" about eight miles north of Gainesville.[85] So productive was the Elrod Mine that in 1833 a North Carolina mining company, already operating a few mines in the area, took out a lease of several years' duration on the property.[86] There were even a few mines opened within the city limits of Gainesville itself.

Another settlement to prosper from the gold rush was Etowah, located about a mile east of where the Canton courthouse is today.[87] When the original Cherokee County was broken up, the area around Etowah retained the name Cherokee, and county elections were scheduled to be held at "the place where John Lay now lives."[88] Early postal records show that the town was called "Cherokee Courthouse" for a time, but in December 1834 it received the name Canton.[89] John P. Brooke, William Grisham, and Joseph Donaldson donated most of the land on which the new town was built.[90] No one knows for sure who suggested the name, but it probably originated with either Grisham or Donaldson. They were both engaged in the silk industry, and it may be that, in a hopeful gesture, they named the town after the great silk producing region around Canton, China.[91]

Canton was from the beginning acknowledged claimant to the county seat and served as the hub of trade and commerce in the Cherokee County area. Gold miners from the surrounding operations sold their findings in the town and bought their supplies there. Two of the wealthiest mines in the area were the Franklin and the Sixes. Gold found at the Cherokee County mines was regarded as "the finest of any in Georgia."[92]

On the southwestern edge of the Cherokee Nation in Carroll County was the small village of Hixville, later named Villa Rica (Spanish for "city of riches"). Though not as prosperous as the richer gold areas to the northeast, Villa Rica attracted considerable attention in 1830 with the discovery of gold on a nearby 200-foot rise called Pine Mountain in Douglas County.[93] Within a short time Villa Rica was a bustling town of two thousand people, several hundred of whom were regularly employed at the mines around Pine Mountain. So highly regarded were the 40-acre gold lots in this area that they sold for between five thousand and twenty thousand dollars each. For several years after the mines opened, their annual output was well over one thousand ounces of gold.[94]

While not as abundant as in areas farther north, gold from the Carroll and Douglas County mines was, according to one claim, "given up to be the purest yet discovered in the United States."[95] In 1833 a man by the name of Jones tunneled sixty feet down to test the feasibility of vein mining on his Pine Mountain property. An eyewitness remembered that the tunnel was "very rich indeed, so much so, that it [was] not uncommon to see particles of gold on the surface of the rocks and find it in great abundance in the dirt thrown out of the vein."[96] Such mining activities, using everything from small cradle rockers to giant stamp mills, became increasingly complex throughout the 1830s as mine owners and investment companies pumped more and more resources into the search for gold.

Chapter Five

"It's Just Like Gambling—All Luck":
Mining in the Gold Rush Days

Though north Georgia towns experienced a population surge in the late 1820s and '30s, most of the people flooding into the region were drawn directly to its gold fields. Armed with pan, pick, and shovel, they roamed the hills and valleys looking for a spot that showed "good color."

Human beings were not the first to extract gold from the Georgia hills. For millions of years the forces of erosion have mined gold in the southern Appalachians. Over the eons wind, rain, freezing, thaw, and plant growth slowly chiseled tons of earth, including gold-bearing quartz veins, from these mountains. As erosion wore the mountains down, new streams containing gold sediments were created, leaving the older, dry creek bottoms behind to form gold-bearing layers embedded in the hills. Early Georgia miners distinguished between these two types by referring to gold found in and along streams as "deposits" and to the older sediments found along the hillsides as "surfaces." These loose particles of gold, whether found along streams or hillsides, are collectively called placers.[1]

Digging for placers was an uncertain business at best. At worst it was a frustrating search, driven by gold fever, that more often than not ended in disappointment. Said Benjamin Parks of gold mining, "It's just like gambling—all luck."[2] But a miner could improve his chances by knowing where to look. Few of the early miners had prior experience at gold digging, but those who stuck with it learned quickly. The best place to test for gold was at a bend in a stream where the eroding bank wall might reveal an ancient gold-bearing gravel layer. When gold is washed from the hillsides into a stream the water's current moves it along. Flakes of gold that do not immediately sink to the bottom are caught at a bend in the creek along with other rock and mineral particles, forming a layer of gravel. The sharper the bend, the more likely gold is to be trapped there.[3] Concerning the origins of these gold-bearing gravels, the geologist and mining engineer William Phillips wrote in 1833, "There are persons who believe that the agent producing them has acted suddenly and that these immense beds of gravel have been collected together at one and the same time. If they reflect, however, they will discover reasons to modify their opinions, and adopt a more plausible and perhaps correct theory."[4] Unlike most of his contemporaries, Phillips understood how gold got where it was as well as how to find it.

When the miners found a spot that showed good color, they set up camp and began working the area in earnest. A variety of crude devices were used to wash these deposits in an effort to extract the fine gold particles. By far the simplest method was panning for gold. Pans varied in size, though the average was around fourteen inches in diameter. A promising scoop of dirt was laid in the pan along with an equal amount of water. The miner then jostled the mixture as the heavy gold flakes worked their way to the bottom. The top layers of soil were periodically allowed to wash over the side, with the miner adding water as needed. Finally, after all the lighter material was washed off, a thin layer of black sand was left at the bottom of the pan. If the gold hunter was lucky, a few brilliant specks of gold could be seen highlighted against the dark surroundings. A skilled miner could go through this process in just a minute or two.[5]

Though the popular image of an early gold miner calls to mind a bearded figure stooped beside a mountain stream looking intently at his pan, the scene was not as typical as one might expect in gold rush Georgia. This method was far too time consuming since only a handful of dirt could be processed at a time. Panning was primarily used in testing soil for gold content and as a final step in more elaborate methods of gold hunting. Panning was also used when it was inconvenient to set up regular equipment at a particular location, especially if the site belonged to someone else. But even with its limitations, the gold pan remained the single most widely used extracting device during the gold rush.

Next to the gold pan, the most popular device in early placer mining was the cradle rocker. The first crude rockers, small half-cylinder wooden troughs into which water and gravel were dumped, were little more that oversized gold pans. A miner would rock the trough back and forth while agitating the mixture by hand, allowing the heavier gold flakes to settle to the bottom. As the gold worked its way down, the miner scraped off the top layers. Eventually, as with the panning process, only a thin layer of black sand, which the miner hoped contained gold, was left at the bottom.

An improved version of the cradle was a wooden box about three feet in length mounted on rockers. Water was poured into the upper end, or hopper, washing gold-bearing gravel through perforations and onto a canvas apron. This apron deflected the gravel to one end of the rocker's lower compartment. Small wooden bars nailed to the bottom of the cradle's open end, called riffle bars, caught sediments containing gold as the gravel washed through.

Another popular device was the sluice box, sometimes called a rippler. This was a simple contraption which consisted of a water flume between ten and twenty feet long containing riffle bars. A continuous flow of water ran through the sluice as miners shoveled in dirt. The flow of water was stopped occasionally, and the gold-bearing sediments were collected and panned out.[6]

The most common examples of gold mining equipment among the Georgia miners were the water flume, the white oak splint basket, and the "gum rocker." These were used in a separating process usually worked by two men. Rich sand and gravel were shoveled into a water flume, through which they were washed down into a splint basket. The basket acted as a screen which allowed only small particles, including the gold, to pass through to the rocker. This was a split, hollowed-out log from six to twelve feet long which was open at both ends. As the gravel washed through the rocker, all the while kept rocking back and forth, the heavier minerals were caught by riffle bars spaced a few inches apart at the bottom of the contraption. As with the sluice box, these sediments were collected periodically, and the gold was panned out.[7]

Another widely used placer mining contraption was the "long tom." Miners shoveled dirt into a water flume, at the end of which was a perforated cast iron plate called a riddle. This riddle served much the same purpose as the splint basket. Sand and gravel washed through the riddle into a riffle box, where the heavy gold particles were trapped behind riffle bars. An improvement on this basic long tom was being used in Georgia by 1833. It consisted of two rectangular boxes, one set above the other, separated by a large riddle. A flume supplied water while a miner stirred dirt in the upper box with a hoe or rake. Holes in the riddle allowed smaller particles of sand and gravel to pass through to the lower box. There riffle bars caught the heavier black sand and gold while the lighter materials washed off.[8]

Still another placer device combined the principles of the long tom and the gum rocker. A flume carried water to a perforated trough, through which it dropped down into a rectangular box containing two compartments separated by a large iron riddle. Use of the perforated trough served to distribute the water more evenly than allowing the water to flow into one end of the box. Dirt and gravel were dumped onto the riddle and agitated with a rake or hoe by one miner. To assist in the agitation, the box, which rested on rollers, was quickly moved back and forth by a second miner. Smaller particles passed through the riddle into a lower compartment containing riffle bars. In this method too, the bars trapped black sand and gold as the lighter material washed away.[9]

Sometimes the riffle bars in all these devices were coated with mercury, or "quicksilver," as the miners called it. This held the gold particles in place while lighter minerals washed away. The use of mercury significantly improved the efficiency of these machines. Even so, the rocker and long tom processes were clumsy and haphazard, the object being not to collect every speck of gold that went through the system but to move as much dirt as possible in a given period of time.[10] Best estimates are that as much as half the deposits worked were lost in this way, and the miners became increasingly concerned about this wastefulness.[11] Wrote one prospector, "So eager are people to find large pieces of gold, that they hurry through the process of washing in a very wasteful manner. . . . We have great need of a few ingenious Yankees to invent labor saving and economical machines for us."[12]

Attempts to improve on existing gold mining technology were made in earnest as the gold rush progressed, and several enterprising souls made more money off the new machines than the miners would make in using them. A man from Clarkesville named T. W. A. Sumter patented, manufactured, and sold what he described as a combined cradle and rocker. By 1831 hundreds of his machines were in use throughout the Southern gold fields.[13] Another device, the Burke Rocker, sold for twenty-five dollars and could process from seven hundred to one thousand bushels of gravel per day.[14] In Auraria John Powell announced that he had applied for patents on two gold-washing machines which, he said, would make the rockers then in use obsolete. Powell claimed that by using the larger of the two machines, eight men could process three hundred bushels of soil in one hour with no loss of gold. He guaranteed that this machine would "wash more grit in a given time than any five machines now in use, and . . . lose less gold than any one."[15]

For those with a bit more money to throw into the search for placer deposits, the north Georgia river bottoms were very attractive. In 1833 miners began drifting flatboats into the Chestatee and Etowah Rivers to bring up rich sand and gravel deposits. These water-borne operations were of various sizes. The most common was worked by two men in a small flatboat about eight to ten feet in length. A specially constructed shovel was driven by a miner into the river bottom near one end of the boat. When the shovel was worked deep enough into the bed, the miner walked to the other end of the boat, bearing down on the handle and loosening the dirt. A second man then drew the gravel to the surface by pulling on a rope attached to the shovel's head. This was repeated, with the men switching functions and working in the opposite direction. Proceeding steadily, two prospectors could make about five loads in a day. One eyewitness recalled seeing a load that yielded more than one-fourth of an ounce of gold, though, he said, the average was much less. On a good day such an operation might bring up from one-half to a full ounce, or about ten to twenty dollars' worth.[16] Some boats were much larger than the eight- to ten-foot average. A good many were so large that it took two men an entire day to fill them using the two-shovel method. These expanded operations were usually worth the effort since, as one Dahlonega resident claimed, the larger loads contained upwards of two ounces of gold worth between forty and fifty dollars.[17]

In early 1833 a large flatboat with a "diving bell" attached was floated into the Chestatee River near Auraria. It was designed and built by a Tennessee engineer named McCollom and by all accounts was very successful. This curiosity was the first of its kind seen in Georgia, and it proved to be quite an attraction. People came from all over the gold region to see the giant dredge in operation.[18] Auraria's "Billy the Poet" immortalized the scene in the *Western Herald*.

> Wend you to the Mines and see,
> The various things for your temptation,
> Stand on the banks of the Chestatee,
> Where the diving bell's in operation.
> Wend you to the pearly stream,
> Where your eyes must be delighted,

Then of golden streets you'll dream,
If perchance you get benighted.[19]

Still more enterprising methods were dreamed up to get at
the rich placer deposits that lay on the river beds. Some miners
with more vision than capital or engineering know-how suggested
draining the rivers to expose the gold-bearing gravel layer. No
such attempt was made in the early nineteenth century, though
Senator John C. Calhoun did invest in a scheme to change the
course of the Chestatee River in an effort to get at the treasures that
lay at its bottom. But the project was canceled when a local "proprietor" refused to allow the proposed channel to cross his land.[20]
Calhoun's enthusiasm for the venture was not recorded, but he
never invested in such an enterprise again.

Despite improvements made on gold-washing machines and
elaborate ideas to get at more of the deposits, placer mining in the
1830s remained somewhat inefficient. The nineteenth-century
mining engineer William Blake estimated that only about a third of
the gold-bearing gravel was ever worked during that era. Of the
deposits that were processed, less than half the gold content was
extracted.[21] So inefficient were the machines that some miners
found they could obtain as much gold by working deposits a
second or even third time as they had gained during the first
processing.[22]

Placer mining was the most popular type among the early
gold diggers because it required very little capital. But as more
people moved into the gold region and towns began to grow,
money became available for investment in vein mining. It was evident to the miners all along that the gold they were panning had
been washed down from gold-bearing quartz veins embedded in
the surrounding hills. When the land lottery ended in 1833 and
land ownership became more settled, miners began prospecting
for the rich gold veins in earnest.

The first vein discoveries were more a result of accident than
of intention, but miners soon became adept at locating gold veins.
Beginning from a spot on a creek or river known to contain placer
deposits, a miner would work his way upstream, testing the soil as
he went. When the soil's gold content dropped abruptly, the miner
knew that there was a vein somewhere in the surrounding hills.
Soil testing would continue until a trail of gold was found that led
up to the vein.[23] It was difficult to tell from these initial tests how
productive a particular vein might turn out to be. The thickness of

veins containing gold ore varied from a few inches to more than twenty feet in some places. These "pinches and swells" occurred with some regularity at a few mines, such as the Franklin, but this was the exception rather than the rule.[24]

The equipment required to conduct vein mining was considerably more complex than that involved in washing placers. Some of the first attempts involved open-pit operations, but most vein mining required the digging of shafts and tunnels. Seven square feet was the recommended size for these tunnels, but most, smaller tunnels operated by one or two miners, were no more than three to four feet in diameter—just large enough for a person to crawl through. Once tunnels were dug, timbers had to be put in place to avert cave-ins. This was particularly important in the Georgia mines because the surrounding rock was riddled with fissures.[25]

Sometimes the miners used pumps or barrels to clear water from the mines, though existing technology made it difficult to attempt mining below the water table.[26] This necessarily limited the depth to which shafts could be sunk. The average mine depth was twenty to thirty feet.[27] The Allatoona Mine in Bartow County was forty feet deep and "quite profitable, as long as the oxidized portion of the vein was worked."[28] One energetic miner who opened more than a hundred mines in Hall, Habersham, and Rabun counties wrote that generally the ore became richer as his shafts descended, "but ceased to be metalliferous at the water level."[29] While admitting that some veins seemed to be less productive below the water table, another writer observed that the mine operators were in general "ignorant of the proper mode of working below the water level."[30] Few mines ran deeper than a hundred feet, and in the years since the gold rush, scarcely more than twenty mines have been sunk below that depth in Georgia.[31] However, there were exceptions, one of the most notable of which was the Loud Mine in White County. At the height of the gold rush it reached a depth of one hundred thirty-five feet.[32]

Hitting the water table was not the only reason mines were sometimes abandoned. Occasionally the veins being followed simply came to an end or became too poor to make mining profitable. The latter was a common occurrence since most operations were relatively small and needed a high profit margin to stay in business. Said one miner, "digging is often abandoned upon the slightest unfavorable appearance such as the narrowing of a vein . . . for there is much . . . disorganization in the veins and rocks.[33]

Where tunnels were dug into the mountainsides, the gold ore was usually hauled out in wheelbarrows. A few of the larger operations laid rail tracks into the mines and brought the ore out in heavy wooden carts.[34] When vertical shafts were sunk, equipment had to be set up to hoist ore to the surface. Rope or cable was run through a pulley suspended over the shaft, and a large bucket or tub was attached and lowered into the hole. Miners working deep in the earth filled these containers with ore, and they were then pulled to the surface by human or horse power. Predictably, the miners generally preferred the use of horses for such work.[35]

Once the gold ore was brought out of the mines, it was crushed almost to powder in a small mortar-and-pestle operation or a larger stamp mill. Stamp mills ranged in size and complexity from a single stamp suspended from a bent-over sapling to mills consisting of ten or twelve stamps driven by a water wheel. The simplest stamp mill was no more than a six-foot oak log between six and eight inches in diameter suspended from a bent-over hickory tree. Using handles attached to either side of the log, one or two men could bring it down with considerable force. When the log was pulled down, a metal plate fastened over its lower end broke up the gold ore. The hickory tree provided enough spring action to lift the log for another descent. Repeated pounding reduced the ore to a fine sand, and the gold was then panned out.[36]

A similar but more elaborate stamp mill consisted of a single such pestle attached to one end of a long horizontal pole. A large bucket was hung on the other end into which a flume poured water. As water filled the bucket, its increasing weight raised the pestle at the opposite end of the pole. At a certain point the bucket hit a peg that dumped the water out and allowed the pestle to crash down on the gold ore. After successive pounding, as in the simpler operation, the gold was panned out.[37]

The larger mining activities built more complex mills containing as many as ten stamps, each weighing anywhere from 100 to 500 pounds.[38] The first of these larger mills was built in 1833 on the banks of Little River at the Columbia Mine, twenty miles west of Augusta in McDuffie County. The three-stamp machine, powered by an undershot water wheel, was owned and operated by a wealthy farmer named Jeremiah Griffin. This was the same man who in 1826 bought three thousand acres along Little River where two English miners claimed to have found gold three years earlier.[39]

These early contraptions were made almost entirely of wood, except for the metal plates attached to each stamp head for crushing the ore. Once a huge squared log was embedded in the ground to serve as a base, upright posts were fitted into this base log about three feet apart and braced. The base log's length and the number of vertical posts fitted into it depended on the number of stamps to be used. Stamp logs about six inches in diameter and eight feet in height were erected between the posts and held in place by a horizontal brace which acted as a guide during the vertical motion of the stamps. Near the middle of each stamp a notch was cut which allowed the stamp to be raised when it was engaged by a peg attached to a rotating horizontal shaft. The shaft was powered by a water wheel that was fed by a canal leading water in from some higher elevation. As the shaft rotated, the peg lifted the stamp and let it fall as the peg rotated out of the notch. The pegs were arranged so that no two stamps fell at the same time. This distributed the load on the shaft and permitted the mill to operate on less power than would otherwise have been possible.[40]

After the crushed ore washed through the mill, it encountered a screen that allowed only fine particles to pass. Material trapped by the screen was collected and fed into the mill a second time. The finer gravel washed over riffled plates lined with mercury to draw out the gold dust in a process called amalgamation. The operators shut the mill down at regular intervals to scrape the gold-bearing mercury from the riffles. This amalgam was then boiled at a temperature of about 400 degrees to separate the gold from the mercury.[41]

Though these stamp mills processed more gold ore than any other method then available, this system was also inefficient. Like the less complex operations, these mills usually allowed more than 50 percent of the raw gold to escape over the mercury plates. One report estimated that these old-style mercury plates sometimes allowed as much as 75 percent of the gold to escape.[42] Another stated that the loss often ran as high as 90 percent.[43] The point is stressed by the observation of a visitor to the gold region who noted that the crushed ore was often run over the mercury plates a second time with considerable profit.[44]

Despite the limitations of the process, mill owners turned a considerable profit since the ore that came out of Georgia was extremely rich. Though the average daily profit was from five to ten pennyweight, some prospectors could boast much more impressive finds. Some of the most productive mines were located along the Sixes Creek in Cherokee County. One report asserted that a single miner took several hundred pennyweight of gold out of one mine in just a few hours. The average for Cherokee County mines, as for those of the entire region, was somewhat lower. The best a miner might hope to make was usually between fifteen and twenty pennyweight of gold per day, or about twenty dollars' worth.[45]

In Gilmer County a man by the name of Zeke Spriggs filled his pockets with so much gold dust from a single day's working at his rocker that his suspenders snapped. One writer insisted that neighbors saw it happen. The place came to be known as Spriggs Hollow, part of the White Path Mining complex.[46] At Pine Mountain in Douglas County the annual yield was around fifty thousand dollars' worth up to 1840.[47] Another rich operation was the Elrod Mine in Hall County. In a single day, September 21, 1830, seven workers took out close to two hundred dollars' worth of pure gold.[48] The Richardson Mine on Duke's Creek, which employed from six to twelve hands, was also noted for its wealth. In 1833 the mine reportedly produced an incredible average of between a hundred and five hundred dollars' worth of gold per day. On one particularly good day eleven workers brought out almost six hundred dollars' worth of gold from this mine.[49] Other White County mines widely known for their productivity were the Williams, Loud, Gordon, Lewis, and Holt.[50]

Some of the most celebrated mines in Georgia were those of Lumpkin County. By far the most famous belonged to John C. Calhoun, from whom the mine took its name. Originally called the O'Barr Mine, it was here that Benjamin Parks said he made his discovery. The property passed through several owners before Calhoun bought the mine for six thousand dollars in June 1833.[51] Calhoun employed twenty hands, and by 1835 the mine was producing close to three dollars a day per hand. Its annual output averaged nearly five hundred dollars per hand.[52] Early in 1833 David Gibson, the man from whom Calhoun bought the property, uncovered a lump of gold ore weighing over nine pounds. According to a report in the *Western Herald*, the rock contained "one hundred and twenty-four particles of gold upon its surface, plainly perceptible to the eye."[53]

One of the most exciting discoveries in Lumpkin County was made in 1833 on the lot of Alfred B. Holt near Auraria. Here a chunk of gold-bearing ore was found that weighed between twenty and thirty pounds and contained "large particles of gold thickly interspersed in it, from the size of a pepper corn to that of a marble." This was, according to *Niles' Register*, considered "an unusual circumstance, gold being almost universally found in grains. The specimen is one of the richest ever seen." It was broken up and sent to Milledgeville and New York, but its owner kept the "finest piece."[54]

These are but a few examples of the wealth produced by the mines of Lumpkin County during the gold rush. According to one "moderate calculation" reported in the *Western Herald,* almost three-quarters of a million dollars' worth of gold was mined in the county during a single season in 1833.[55] John C. Calhoun himself wrote in 1835 that gold mining activities in Lumpkin were "universally doing well. I could not hear of an instance of unsuccessful operation, when I was [there]; and some were doing most extraordinary business."[56] Georgia's gold mining industry was so lucrative in the 1830s that one Lumpkin County resident was led to ask, "What Cotton growing county in the state can compete with us?"[57]

The development of vein mining was spurred on by newspaper editorials expounding its merits and pointing out that the placer deposits would eventually give out.[58] Wrote one gentleman who traveled through the gold belt in 1833, "The deposits will be exhausted in three or four years, and the veins must be the places of permanent operation in the Gold Region."[59]

Following their advice, mining companies began forming in Habersham County as early as 1832. Some of the earliest included the Augusta Mining Company, the Habersham Mining Company, and the Naucoochy Mining Company, all chartered in December of that year.[60] Within a short time the state was regularly granting charters to such ventures as the Cherokee Mining Company, the Chestatee Mining Company, the Belfast Mining Company, the Canton Mining Company of Georgia, and the Lumpkin County Mining and Manufacturing Company.[61]

These early mining companies were often formed by small groups of well-to-do Georgians who saw gold mining as more than a passing fad. The Chestatee Mining Company, incorporated by the General Assembly in 1835, was one such firm. Its charter members, Charles M'Donald, Farish Carter, and Henry M. Clay, were authorized to offer up to one hundred thousand dollars' worth of stock to the public. They were also empowered to draw up a constitution for the company provided that its dictates were not contrary to the laws of Georgia or the United States. The company directors were to be elected annually on the first Tuesday in December, with each share of stock entitling its owner to one vote. The election would be supervised by two justices of the peace who were not stockholders. The sitting directors would determine the

Heart of the Gold Region

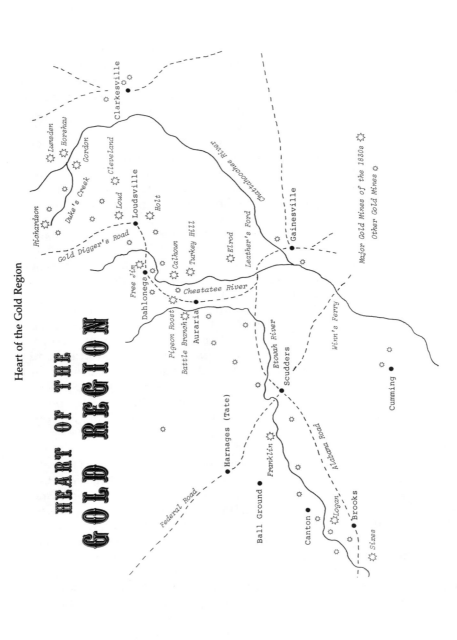

HEART OF THE
GOLD REGION

Clarkesville

☆ Lumsden
☆ Horshaw
☆ Gordon
☆ Cleveland
Richardson ☆
Duke's Creek
☆ ☆ Loud Loudsville
☆ ☆ Holt
Gold Digger's Road
Free Jim ☆
Dahlonega ●
☆ Calhoun
☆ Turkey Hill
Chestatee River
☆ Elrod
Leather's Ford
Chattahoochee River
Gainesville ●
☆
Pigeon Roost ☆
Battle Branch ☆
Auraria
☆
Etowah River
Scudders ●
Winn's Ferry
Harnages (Tate) ●
☆
Franklin ☆
☆
Alabama Road
Ball Ground ●
Federal Road
Canton ●
☆Logan
Brooks ●
☆
☆ Sixes
Cumming ●

☆ Major Gold Mines of the 1830s
☆ Other Gold Mines

time and place of the annual meetings and give thirty days' notice thereof in one or more area newspapers.[62] The organization and regulations of the Chestatee Mining Company were typical of those incorporated in Georgia.

The value of stock in these companies ranged from one hundred thousand to a million dollars. Sources of capital included wealthy Southerners, Northern financial establishments, and foreign investors. At least one writer suggests that most of this investment capital was provided by foreigners, though there is some room for doubt on this point.[63] Even so, it is certain that a large percentage of mining capital originated overseas. In a strong vein of nativism one editorial writer called foreign involvement in Georgia's mines a "vulgar error" and lamented that foreigners made any profit whatever from the American gold mining industry.[64]

Numerous advertisements appeared in Georgia newspapers offering the services of agents who could secure capital investments for those wishing to expand their mining operations. Typical of such notices was the following ad placed by James F. D. Oldenburg of New York City in an 1831 issue of the *Macon Advertiser*:

> To Owners of Gold Mines
> The subscriber respectfully informs those owners of property in the South, that his acquaintance with the American, Foreign, and Emigrant Capitalists, is very extensive—and so many are constantly communicating by letter and in person, making inquiry how they may invest their funds to good advantage, wishing to know if some plan could not be adopted, that they might communicate and correspond with owners of Mines.

Oldenburg's fee was ten dollars on an investment of twenty thousand dollars and twenty dollars for one of fifty thousand.[65] Such business was quite lucrative, for the total amount of stock sales by the mid-1830s was estimated at fifty million dollars. Some returns on the New York exchange went as high as 20 percent.[66]

Three of the most successful gold mining companies were the Belfast Mining Company, the Pigeon Roost Mining Company, and the mining firm of Ware and Matthews. In the spring of 1834 Ware and Matthews erected a stamp mill and sunk mine shafts up to 100 feet in depth, making it one of the largest operations in the gold region.[67] The Belfast Mining Company, chartered that same year with five hundred thousand dollars' worth of stock, was one of the best backed mines in Georgia. Perhaps the largest of the gold rush mining operations was the Pigeon Roost Mining Company. Formerly the Jefferson Company, it owned four of the richest 40-acre gold lots in Lumpkin County. In 1835 the company put a stock offer of four hundred thousand dollars before the public, and one newspaper insisted that stock taken in the company would be "far more valuable than in any institution in the United States."[68]

In addition to investors who wished to profit from mining ventures, there were those who hoped to make money by buying gold lots and reselling them at higher prices. Georgia newspapers were littered with advertisements of land speculators offering to buy or sell gold mines. Thomas Butler King of Glynn County on the Georgia coast bought at least twenty-seven gold lots and offered them for sale in November 1833.[69] The rate at which some mines changed hands was astounding. Lot 747 in Lumpkin County was granted by the lottery wheel to Martin Strother of Newton County in 1832. By 1835 the entire lot, or parts of it, had changed hands no fewer than twelve times.[70]

To aid those engaged in the exchange of mines, the *Federal Union* printed and sold a publication entitled "Gold Lottery Lists," which sold for five dollars.[71] Scores of local residents and a few knowledgeable mining engineers offered to test gold lots and give written estimates of their value. Colonel D. C. Gibson of Auraria gave notice that for a fee of twenty-five dollars he would test any lot in the gold region and give a written guarantee of his estimate.[72] With assistance such as this, speculation was so widespread that one paper complained, "Mining in Georgia has not yet assumed a fixed character. Those who have been engaged in it have made it rather a matter of speculation, by frequent transfers, than to ascertain the real value on the property. Hence so many frauds practiced upon the inexperienced and credulous."[73]

As the writer of this article suggests, land speculation was not always of the honest variety. It was not uncommon for a gold lot to be put up for sale by a person whose claim to it was questionable if not outright fraudulent. Most dishonest speculators, the smarter ones anyway, went by assumed names and made themselves scarce immediately after the sale. By the time an unknowing buyer discovered that he had been cheated, it was usually too late to do anything about it. In advertisements offering his twenty-seven lots for sale, Thomas Butler King listed them by number and warned interested persons against buying them from speculators who might claim to be their owners.[74] Even legitimate owners sometimes planted gold nuggets on their property to artificially increase its value.[75] Though the primary reason for the mining industry's sharp decline in the 1840s was simply that the gold began to play out, Fletcher Green points out that "the spirit of dishonest speculation contributed a great deal to the failure of the [gold] mining industry since it frightened away much needed capital."[76]

Fear of dishonest speculation persisted for some time after the gold rush. In 1857 what would become known as the Findley Chute was discovered by a man hired by J. J. Findley to test for gold. Findley doubted the title of the man who claimed to own the lot (number 1048) and anticipated trouble in getting the right to work it. He took on Harrison Riley as a partner in the venture, and the two men immediately set to work. However, they were understandably careful not to let news of their find become widely known.[77]

The excitement produced in the 1830s by the discovery of gold in Georgia was due as much to the quality of this precious metal as to its quantity. The purity of Georgia gold was renowned during the gold rush and remains so to this day. Even now Southern gold is said to be some of the world's finest, rivaled only by that found in Australia. Gold that is 70 parts per 100 pure is normally considered profitable to mine. Georgia gold averages about 95 percent pure and is rarely less than 90 percent as compared with the 88 percent average of gold found in California and Alaska.[78] Gold found in the immediate vicinity of Auraria is reportedly the purest to be had in the Georgia gold region, averaging 95 percent.[79]

One of the finest nuggets ever discovered came from the Southern gold fields and was found to be 99.4 percent free of impurities.[80] Said one enthusiastic newspaper of Georgia's gold, "It proves to be virgin gold, as pure as that precious metal can be, and more so than the gold coin in circulation, which has in its composition a certain portion of alloy."[81] In 1844 Thomas G. Clemson observed that "a mere glance of the eye is frequently sufficient to . . . fix its value. The gold taken from the Chestatee River has a smooth, clean, glossy appearance, something like flax seed."[82]

Once this gold was panned out or separated from its ore, it was often used as a direct medium of exchange. Miners carried gold dust in goose quills and small pouches or simply loose in their vest pockets.[83] On Saturday afternoons they took their gold into town and sold it to the storekeepers or traded it for merchandise.[84] Taverns were very popular among the miners, and they spent much of their gold in these establishments. Some of the gold made its way to Tennessee and Kentucky in exchange for livestock brought to the gold region by drovers from those states. Gold was also sold to individuals and bankers at very low rates.[85] Because of its fineness, Georgia gold was popular for making jewelry and was also in demand as an export commodity.[86]

A substantial portion of the gold was sent to the federal mint in Philadelphia. Between 1830 and 1837 the mint received $1,798,900 in gold from the Georgia mines.[87] When gold was brought to the mint, the treasurer issued a certificate testifying to its value and stating the amount in gold coin to be paid for it. If the owner wished, he could present the certificate at the Bank of the United States in Philadelphia and receive the amount of gold stated thereon or he could wait for his own gold to be minted. The former option was usually preferred since it might take as long as three months for raw gold to be returned as coin. If the owner did not want to make the trip to Philadelphia, he could deposit his bullion at branch banks in Charleston or Savannah. However, he would be paid no more than two-thirds of the gold's estimated value at the time of deposit. The balance would be paid when the bullion's value was fixed by the mint, a process which sometimes took several months.[88]

There were obvious problems associated with delivering gold to the federal mint. If a miner chose to make the journey, it took considerable time and there was always the danger of being robbed. Even dealing with a branch bank was inconvenient since two trips were required to receive the gold's full value. If a miner did not want to barter his gold or sell it locally for a price that was usually lower than its actual value, his only option was to take the gold to a privately owned mint.[89]

Some took their gold to Christopher Bechtler in Rutherfordton, North Carolina, near that state's South Mountain gold district. Bechtler stamped a series of one-, two-and-a-half-, and five-dollar gold pieces that were slightly finer than gold coins put out by the Philadelphia mint. Between 1831 and 1840 the Bechtler mint issued the equivalent of $3,625,840 in gold coins and certified ingots, making it the most productive private mint in United States history.[90]

Though Bechtler's was more successful, the first mint to serve the Southern gold fields was owned and operated by a German immigrant named Templeton Reid. In 1830 Reid, a gunsmith and clock maker by trade, established a mint in Milledgeville. The July 24 issue of the *Southern Recorder* announced that "about $1,500 worth of Georgia Gold has been stamped by our ingenious townsman, Mr. Templeton Reid. . . . Mr. Reid informs us that the gold thus stamped by him, will be taken at the mint and at most of the Banks for the value it purports on its face to bear."[91] By September of that year Reid had moved his mint to Gainesville, where he coined two-and-a-half-, five-, and ten-dollar gold pieces. This was exactly what the miners needed—a place to exchange their gold for coin at a not too distant location. One newspaper wrote that the Gainesville mint "will be a great convenience and saving to the miners, who have heretofore been obliged to part with the precious metal in its crude state at a loss of from five to fifteen per cent."[92]

Despite the initial popularity of Reid's mint, it remained in operation only a short time. His troubles began in August 1830 with a letter to the editor of the *Georgia Courier* announcing that Reid's coins had been assayed at the mint in Philadelphia and found to be worth less than their face value.[93] Reid responded with his own letter defending the value of his coins, but the damage to his reputation was already done. Public confidence in Reid was gone, and he was forced to close down by the end of the year.[94]

As it turned out, Reid's coins were indeed worth less than face value. It seems Reid failed to take into account the impurities such as silver and tin alloyed with gold in its natural state. An 1835 article in *The American Journal of Science and Arts* reported that an analysis of a Reid ten-dollar gold piece revealed a purity of 95.579 percent, the remainder being silver.[95] But Reid had assumed the purity of raw gold to be at least 99 percent and stamped his coins accordingly.[96] Though apparently Reid was, in the words of one writer, "more ignorant than greedy," it was a mistake that proved fatal to his business.[97]

During its short existence, Reid's mint may have produced as many as fifteen hundred coins with a face value of approximately six thousand dollars.[98] These coins are extremely rare today not only because so few were minted but also because most of them were melted down in the 1830s when they were found to be worth less than face value. The Smithsonian Institution has one full set, and another is in private hands. At best estimate there are probably no more than six pieces of each issue in existence.[99] So scarce are the coins that in 1979 a Reid five-dollar gold piece, once ridiculed as worth only $4.69, sold for two hundred thousand dollars at auction.[100] Ironically, Reid complained that even at the height of its operation his mint barely turned a profit.

If Templeton Reid found it difficult to prosper in Georgia's gold region, he was far from alone. While a few miners did strike it rich, they were the rare exceptions. The majority were fortunate simply to make a living. Most often the people who made their fortune in the gold fields were the merchants—those who mined the miners. As Benjamin Parks said, and as every miner knew, to hit a gold-rich vein or placer deposit was all a matter of luck.

Chapter Six

"Gambling Houses, Dancing Houses, & Drinking Saloons":
Life in the Georgia Gold Region

The people who worked the placer and vein mines were a varied lot. Some roamed the countryside searching for deposits while others leased mines or bought them outright. When those who owned gold lots leased their property, it was usually in exchange for between one-tenth and one-half of the gold mined. The typical agreement granted one-fourth of the gold production to the landowner. In some instances, especially when absentee landowners were involved, "a standing joke among the miners [was] that they had left the rent in the ground and the owners could get it themselves whenever they wanted it bad enough."[1]

Some miners did not even bother to inform the owners that they were digging on their land. It was not very difficult to get away with mining on someone else's land in the early days of the gold rush, especially during and immediately following the lottery when land ownership was often in doubt. This practice, known appropriately as "swindling," was so common along one creek that it was called Swindling Branch.[2]

Mining was very popular as an off-season activity among those whose primary occupation was agriculture. After the fall harvest, many farmers and planters headed for the hills to try their luck in the gold fields. Those who were residents of the gold country often operated mines on their own lands as an adjunct to farming.[3] There were also planters who bought or leased gold lands and worked slaves in the mines seasonally or throughout the year.[4] Others gave up "King Cotton" and devoted themselves entirely to gold mining.[5] As one writer put it, "Where mining proved more profitable than planting, the former superseded the latter entirely."[6] In most cases, however, when the price of cotton was high, farmers and planters abandoned the gold fields, but they returned to the mines when the price of cotton again fell off.[7]

As epidemic as gold fever was in the region, there were at least a few farmers who successfully resisted the disease. Edward Williams of Nacoochee Valley, known to all as "Major," was among this number. Though he was a close friend of John C. Calhoun, who often stayed at the Williams residence while visiting his Georgia mines, the major did not share Calhoun's enthusiasm for gold digging. But stories of gold nuggets worth from five hundred to twenty thousand dollars were more than enough to fire the imagination of the major's twelve-year-old son George. The boy was probably also influenced by Calhoun, for whom he served as a guide around Nacoochee Valley. Whatever the source of his infection, young George had a bad case of gold fever. Day after day he earnestly pleaded with his father to let him do some mining on the side. One day, to the boy's surprise, the major agreed, saying they would start first thing in the morning. George was so excited that he got little sleep that night because, as he put it, "visions of gold dazzled my wakeful eyes." The next morning the major took his anxious son out to the barn, told him to harness the plow horse, "Old Dick," and said, "Now George, you see the corn before you, plow four furrows carefully between each row. This field is a sure gold mine—one that has never failed me. We will make corn to sell to those men who spend all their time hunting for gold." By the end of the day George was, as he put it, "too tired and too little fanciful to dream; by morning the gold fever was so effectively cured, I have never had a return of it."[8]

Major Williams's antipathy to gold mining was the exception to the rule among north Georgia farmers. Most were eager to try their luck in the gold fields. This practice was so common that the nineteenth-century mining engineers Nitze and Wilkens commented that "Farming and gold-digging went, in many cases, hand in hand. When crops were laid by, the slaves and farm-hands were turned into the creek-bottoms, thus utilizing their time during the dull season."[9] One man from Augusta named Phinizy brought a large group of slaves to the gold region each summer to work in the mines.[10] Thomas Lumsden, who owned a mine in Nacoochee Valley, recorded that his slaves produced thirty thousand dollars in gold during a single season.[11] At one point John C. Calhoun had at least twenty slaves working in his mine.[12] Slaves were also purchased for work in the mines or leased from plantation owners for that purpose. Advertisements in Georgia newspapers gave notice to slave traders that "Liberal prices will be given for Negroes."[13] Such ads also announced that "Strong Negro Men are in demand at the Mines, at $10 per month."[14] The money, of course, went to the slave's owner.

The slaves quite naturally resented not profiting from their own labor. Some sought to compensate themselves by concealing what gold they could from the overseer. They hid it in the seams of their clothing and even placed gold dust and small nuggets in their hair. This practice was common among free miners as well, though not always successful. One mine proprietor surprised his workers one evening by ordering that they be shaven before going to their quarters. When the hair was shaken out, several ounces of pure gold were recovered.[15]

Sometimes while working in the mines slaves attempted to bury gold nuggets secretly and retrieve them at a more opportune time. One Gilmer County slave maneuvered a large nugget from his shovel and worked it into the dirt with his foot when no one was watching. That night he escaped and tried to find his treasure, but the mine was pitch black. The unfortunate slave found it impossible to locate the spot where had buried the nugget. While he was vainly searching for what might have been a ticket to freedom, his absence was detected and he was severely beaten for his "insolence." The nugget was later found and estimated to be worth over six hundred dollars.[16]

When slaves were successful in concealing gold from their owners, they usually tried to sell it to the first convenient buyer. This was risky business both for the buyer and the seller. In 1833 the Lumpkin County Grand Jury brought charges against Jefferson Witherow, Alfred Witherow, and Frances B. Bulfinch for buying ten dollars' worth of gold from the slaves of James H. Poteet, Jacob Page, and Leander Smith.[17] In Habersham County a white man named Andrew Johnson was charged with "trading with a slave." Johnson pled guilty and was fined five dollars.[18]

There were at least a few slaves who did not have to conceal gold from their masters. Some mine owners allowed their slaves to keep a portion of the gold they discovered while others rented out slaves and let them have a percentage of the proceeds. Jacob Scudder permitted his slaves to keep all the gold they found after sundown at his placer mine. It was, of course, no easy task to find tiny bits of gold in the dark by pine torchlight, but Scudder placed no limit on the amount of gold they could pan. However, he did insist that they sell their findings only to him. A few of his slaves saved enough gold from their nightly workings to purchase their freedom.[19]

In addition to hard work and brutal treatment, the mines also presented a danger to both life and limb for the slaves. Many tunnels were hastily dug and haphazardly braced by inexperienced workers. It is not surprising that such tunnels were subject to cave-ins without warning. This was a constant danger to all mine workers, slave or free. An entire work gang of slaves was once killed when supporting timbers gave way and the roof collapsed at the Franklin Mine in Cherokee County.[20]

Besides the more obvious dangers, some slaves were faced with an additional burden imposed by the leasing system. Mine owners frequently leased slaves from low-country planters, especially during fall and winter months after the crops were laid by. This proved especially hazardous for the slaves since mine operators had no great financial stake in their well-being. As a consequence, leased slaves were poorly fed and frequently worked to death. One visitor to the Georgia gold region described their appearance as "exhausted, squalid, and sickly."[21] The death rate among valuable slaves grew so high that planters became wary of leasing out their "property." Calhoun refused to lease his slaves for work in the mines and advised others to do likewise.

Many north Georgia slaves found their treatment and the dangers of mining so unbearable that, like thousands of others in the antebellum South, they decided to run away. A few slaves used the gold they had hidden to help them get out of the South once they made a break for it. Area newspapers carried notices calling for the return of runaway slaves, sometimes offering handsome rewards. A Cass County mine owner, Charles Cleghorn, announced in the Western Herald that a slave named Jack escaped from his Allatoona Mine. Cleghorn offered fifty dollars for his return "or twenty-five dollars if lodged in any Jail." Jack was a blacksmith by trade and described as heavy built and "light complected, but a full blooded negro." He had "a down look when spoken to," spoke "slow and somewhat stammering," and was "very fond of spirits."[22]

Another slave, named Henry, apparently unhappy with his treatment, escaped from a gold mine owned by Nathan Cook on the outskirts of Auraria. Cook thought that eighteen-year-old Henry might be headed for North Carolina, where he had lived before being brought to Georgia by a speculator. Henry was described as a tall man and, like the slave Jack, had "rather a down look, when spoken to." A reward was offered to anyone who could capture and hold Henry.[23] "A Negro Fellow by the name of John," who had worked in Auraria as a cook in the taverns of William

Rogers and Robert A. Watkins, ran away from the mining operations of a man named Pinchback in October 1833. It is hardly surprising that John was much more fond of cooking than of mining. Pinchback offered a ten dollar reward to get John back.[24]

There were also advertisements announcing the capture of African Americans thought for one reason or another to be escaped slaves. Typical of these is the following item from an April 1833 issue of the *Southern Banner:*[25]

Notice

Brought to Clayton Jail, Rabun county, on Tuesday the fifth instant, a mulatto fellow who says he is a free man, and was hired to P. Caldwell at the gold mines in Lumpkin, and was raised by James Campbell of Iredell county, North Carolina. The owner is requested to come and pay charges, and take him away.

T. M. HENSON,
Jailer

It is not known what cause the jailer had to doubt this man's claim to freedom other than the color of his skin. In antebellum Georgia, where less than one percent of the African-American population was free, that was usually enough.[26]

But not all African Americans in the gold region were slaves. Though few in number, there were "free persons of color" who farmed or worked in the mines. A good many did both. This was the case with Dan and Lucinda Riley, who bought their freedom from Jacob Scudder. After their emancipation, the couple worked as sharecroppers and panned for gold in the vicinity of the Franklin Mine to supplement their income.[27]

Despite the ability of some African Americans in the Georgia gold region to buy their way out of slavery, it is important to note that most were taken there as slaves and remained slaves. The number of slaves involved in this forced labor is still uncertain. Since most slaves were used as transient labor, this is and must remain and open question. It can be said, however, that although some mine owners found it quite profitable to use slaves, the practice was not nearly as common in the gold mines of north Georgia as it was on cotton and rice plantations of the coastal plains. Local white residents were uncomfortable with the presence of a large slave population in the vicinity, and mine operators usually preferred free labor anyway. It was cheap and did not incur the responsibilities of food, clothing, and shelter associated with slavery.[28]

The use of slaves in gold mining decreased sharply in the 1840s as the gold began to play out. Within a few years, hardly any slaves were left in the mines. After their emancipation in the 1860s, African Americans became so scarce in north Georgia that an 1886 issue of the *Dahlonega Signal* claimed there were whites living in the mountains just eighteen miles north of town who had never seen a person of African descent.[29]

Mining companies or individual owners who preferred white labor had little trouble finding it. Many prospectors who had been working the gold deposits sought work in large vein mines as the placers became more scarce. Some miners even used area newspapers to advertise their desire for employment in the mines. One Auraria man, an experienced miner with good references, gave notice in the *Western Herald* that he wished "to get employment in a mine, vein or deposit."[30] To help supply the demand for mine workers, one man built a stockade and leased convicts to mining companies.[31] Of course white labor, whether free or convict, also had its problems. Mine workers were frequently caught trying to sneak gold out of the mines. At one mine the workers' official wage was one dollar and fifty cents a day, but some managed to average as much as five dollars by "holding back."[32]

The gold rush also attracted a good many foreigners to Georgia. They were mainly natives of Germany, Sweden, Switzerland, Spain, England, Scotland, Ireland, and Wales. Many had previous experience in the mines of Europe and South America.[33] Two brothers from Ireland who "understood the science of digging to perfection" leased one or two lots around Dahlonega and within a few years were worth approximately fifteen thousand dollars.[34]

With so many people pouring into the area, and with the Cherokees holding steadfast to their claim on the land, there were bound to be conflicts over the mines. One of the most violent occurred near Scudder's Inn in Forsyth County when about thirty Cherokees and a like number of whites battled with "fists, sticks and stones." No one was killed, but there were a number of black eyes and broken bones.[35]

Several weeks later another serious dispute broke out at a mine in Lumpkin County. According to a contemporary newspaper account,[36]

> Messrs. Bolton and Lindsey had purchased the lot which gave rise to the difficulty; and that Lindsey went in possession with a company of twelve or fourteen hands and commenced operating for gold. Our informant also states that there was an Indian house on the lot, and that an Indian by the name of Bean claimed the possession of it, and forbid [sic] Lindsey's right to it. Lindsey paid no at-

tention to him until . . . on Tuesday last, the war whoop was raised from the house on the lot, and about twenty-five or thirty Indians all painted and undressed, rushed out and continued the yell of war, until they got in proper distance of the white men on the branch, and attacked them with sticks, clubs and rocks. The whites defended themselves with their mining tools; the contest was kept up about two hours. A white man, by the name of Goodwin, lately from Kentucky, got his arm broken in two places, and six or seven Indians [were] dangerously wounded. The whites are still in possession.

Another rather unusual confrontation occurred when "an almost nude Indian woman of powerful frame" attacked a group of miners who were digging along a stream near Dahlonega. She jumped down into their pit and put up such a fight that the miners felt lucky to escape with their lives. In commemoration of the event this stream came to be called Amazon Branch.[37]

Still other battles took place between gangs of white miners fighting for possession of choice gold property. On one occasion sixty Carolinians set upon a group of twenty Georgians. When the attackers were finally driven off, one man was mortally injured and others were seriously hurt.[38] In May 1831 a confrontation developed on a small tributary of the Etowah River. An argument over property rights broke out between a group of miners from Tennessee, who had probably come to the region to trade as well as hunt for gold, and a party of Georgians. The dispute quickly turned violent and several men were badly injured. According to some reports, at least one man was killed. To this day the place is known as Battle Branch. Major John Hockenhull later owned the Battle Branch Mine and by all accounts worked it very profitably. After about 1840, when Hockenhull retired to a farm in Dawson County, the mine continued to produce a good income for its new owner, a man by the name of John Pasco.[39]

In addition to disputes over mining rights, the swelling population caused other problems. The first difficulty encountered by travelers making their way to north Georgia was simply getting to the gold region. Horseback was the most common mode of transportation, and the area's isolation sometimes made travel a lonely experience. The novelist William Gilmore Simms wrote this impression of his journey through north Georgia in the early 1830s: "All around, far as the eye may see, it looks in vain for relief in variety. There still stretch the dreary wastes, the dull woods, the long sandy tracts, and the rude hills that send out no voices, and hang out no lights. . . . " Still, Simms found much to be admired in these rolling hills, where, as he put it, "sun and sky do their work of beauty upon earth, without heeding the ungracious return which she may make; and a rich warm sunset flung over the hills and woods a delicious atmosphere of beauty, burnishing the dull heights and the gloomy pines with golden hues, far more bright, if far less highly valued by men, than the metallic treasures which lay beneath their masses."[40]

But such visions were usually lost on those passing through this rugged gold country. There were few roads, and these were usually in poor condition. Typical of the miners' attitude and experience was this quote from a Loudsville man dated December 23, 1833: "It has been raining, snowing, and hailing here for the last week . . . The roads are almost impossible. You know when this country is in its most flourishing condition, [it] is not overly pleasant."[41] A visitor to the gold region wrote of an 1833 trip from Athens to Clarkesville "in a clumsy stage, rumbling and jolting over intolerable roads."[42] Despite the bad roads, a number of stage lines were established in an attempt to keep north Georgia in touch with the outside world. These included a twice-weekly service between Pendleton, South Carolina (Calhoun's home district), and Gainesville, and a line that ran from Athens to "Lumpkin County Courthouse" three times a week.[43]

If transportation was rough and unpredictable, the hotels and taverns that sprang up across the region, though not luxurious, were at least comfortable. The proprietor of the Troup Hotel in Clarkesville ran an ad in Georgia newspapers boasting "of as spacious, commodious and pleasant an establishment, as any in the up-country of Georgia."[44] One early traveler wrote of the Dahlonega hotels, "the comforts for the inner man were not excelled by any in the State."[45]

One of the most popular of the area's hotels was run by Agnes Paschal, or "Grandma" Paschal, as she was affectionately called by the folks in and around Auraria.[46] In January 1833 one of her sons, George Washington Paschal, moved to Auraria and set up a law office. He soon purchased the hotel and tavern owned by Nathaniel Nuckolls, and in April the *Western Herald* announced the opening of "Mrs. Paschal and Sons." The paper assured potential customers that they would receive as good accommodations here as any in the country.[47] Later that year they moved to "the new framed building in the north end of this town" and promised "to entertain in a comfortable manner, all persons who may give them a call."[48] Though Grandma Paschal allowed no liquor in her establishment, it was still very popular with visitors to the gold region. Important civic meetings were often held there, and Calhoun made the Paschal Inn a regular stop on his visits to Auraria.[49]

So many people moved into north Georgia so quickly that there were shortages of almost everything. Of particular concern to the residents was the scarcity of food. An April 1833 edition of Auraria's *Western Herald* encouraged farmers to bring their business to the area: "The infancy of the country, and the consequent scarcity of provisions, affords inducements to the agriculturalists of the adjacent counties, to look to this as a market for their surplus produce." To lure farmers and their foodstuffs to the gold region, the *Herald* listed current prices on the following items, adding that they were "in much demand in this market."[50]

Corn—75 to 87½ cents per bushel
Meal—87½ cents to $1.00 per bushel
Fodder—$2.50 to $3.00 per hundred pounds
Flour—$10.00 per barrel
Butter—18¾ to 25 cents per pound
Chickens—12½ to 18¾ cents per pound
Vegetables—"In proportion"

By October 1833 prices had not changed much, but these additional items were listed: "Eggs—12½ to 18¾ cents per dozen, Potatoes—50 to 75 cents per bushel, and Turnips—25 to 37½ cents per bushel".[51]

Of all the food products sought after in the gold region, the one most in demand was meat. So scarce was this commodity that at one point there was not a single pound of bacon for sale in all of Lumpkin County.[52] To satisfy the demand for meat, drovers from as far away as Tennessee and Kentucky brought their livestock to the Georgia gold country. Hundreds of hogs, sheep, cattle, and even turkeys and ducks were driven down the Federal Road year-round.[53]

The mining settlements had slaughter pens on their outskirts to accommodate the drovers when they came to town. As late as the 1930s the remains of Auraria's slaughter pens from one hundred years before could still be seen. The drovers' arrival was always looked forward to as an exciting event in the gold region. Townspeople turned out to watch the spectacle and to get a bargain on meat when the slaughter began. Pork could be bought for as little as two and a half cents a pound since what parts the

The Gold Deposits of Georgia

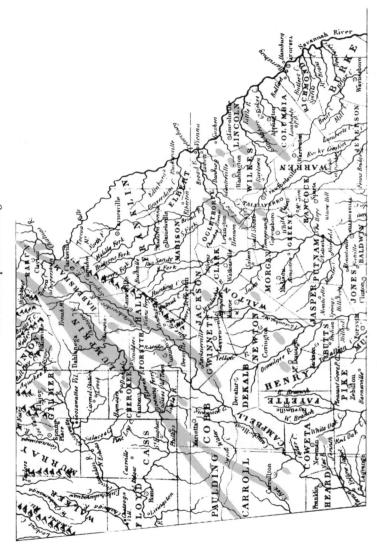

miners did not buy had to be hauled southward and sold in the larger towns like Milledgeville and Augusta. There was also money to be made for the more industrious folk. Women often took contracts to render lard "on halves," that is, to boil hog fat down to lard in exchange for half of the product. Some stored up enough lard in this way to last a whole year.[54]

One of the most entertaining sights for the people of Georgia's gold region was the turkey drive. It was hard enough to manage the turkeys during daylight hours, but when evening came it was impossible to keep them from flying in all directions looking for a convenient tree in which to roost. Since there was no way to continue the drive after nightfall, drovers did their best to reach designated roosting stations along the route before dark. Almost every north Georgia town had such a station in the vicinity. If the next station could not be reached by evening, the turkeys could not be expected to cooperate with the efforts of their drovers to keep them together. The turkeys could also prove stubborn in the mornings just after daybreak. If the drovers were not careful, their stock would scatter into the surrounding woods and fields, and it might take all day to round them up. Even then a good many would be lost. There were usually hundreds of turkeys involved in these drives. With so many in stock, the prices were generally low, especially during rainy weather, when it was difficult to reach the next roosting station by dark.[55]

The native Cherokees also provided meat and other foodstuffs for the miners. Groups of Cherokee hunters could occasionally be seen riding into town with loads of deer meat and wild turkey. Sometimes they brought in honey as well. They sold their goods directly to the miners for cash or bartered with local merchants for the items they needed.[56]

To deal with the scarcity not only of food but of every type of consumer item, merchants set up shops all across the gold region. A. M'Laughlin and Company established a wholesale venture in Auraria to encourage businessmen to establish themselves in the area. They had four thousand dollars in merchandise, mostly groceries and dry goods, and ran ads in the local newspaper to encourage businessmen to establish themselves in the area, inviting those "wishing to embark in the business in the Gold Region, and in a populous and flourishing Village . . . to call without delay at the Store, and examine for themselves."[57]

One of the best-supplied stores in all of north Georgia was that of S. T. Rowland in Auraria. In an April 1833 issue of the

Western Herald Rowland announced receipt of a large shipment "of Dry-Goods, Groceries, Hardware & Crockery" from New York and Charleston. The ad is particularly interesting because the dozens of items listed give an insight into what a miner could purchase with his gold. Rowland included such goods as diapers, calico, "Turkey Red Prints," shawls, Irish linen, "Satinett, Silk & Cotton Flag," ready-made clothing, and handkerchiefs as well as 4,000 yards of "Sheeting and Shirting" and 2,000 yards of "Cheap Negro Cloth." He also had molasses, St. Croix sugar, coffee, cognac, peach brandy, champagne, claret, port, New Orleans and New England rum, Holland gin, Madeira wine, soap, rice, crackers, mackerel, sperm candles, almonds, herring, tobacco, raisins, spades, shovels, blacksmith tools, saws, nails, window glass, knives and forks, "Pocket, Pen and Dirk Knives," razors, scissors, shears, locks, rifles, shotguns, pencils, pens, carpenter tools, china and glassware, axes, tea kettles, tinware, wool hats, fur hats, and 5,000 "Spanish Segars." Rowland also gave notice that he would purchase gold and give the highest prices for it.[58]

Another Auraria establishment, H. C. & G. C. Bradford's, received its goods from Baltimore and Philadelphia and carried almost as many items as Rowland's. Additionally they had in stock "Chissels, Augers, Handsaws and Hammers, Hinges, Waffle Irons, Grid Irons," and "Shoes and Boots."[59] Auraria also had a confectionery shop, owned and operated by John H. Ware. He promised to have in stock all items that might be expected at such an establishment, but warned, "You who call must not expect to find me in a fine Building, still you will find the best of articles. . . ."[60] The town had a tinsmith named A. Johnson who built a tin factory and sold all kinds of tinware at wholesale or retail.[61]

While some businesses offered merchandise in exchange for "Cash or Gold," others had only their services to render. There were several tailors in Auraria alone. The shop of D. A. Wiles and W. S. Sanders received the latest New York and Philadelphia fashions and gave "every pledge on their part to please the fancy and tastefully fit all those who patronize them in their business."[62] Wiles also operated a shop under his name alone, announcing monthly fashions from New York, Philadelphia, and Baltimore and hoping "from assiduous attention to business to merit a share of public patronage."[63] J. J. Land, another tailor, declared that "if strict attention to business, and good work" would give him a share of the public patronage, then he meant to have it.[64] And

B. C. Candee guaranteed his work "to be equal to that done in Augusta, or elsewhere."[65]

Barbers too practiced their trade in gold country. One clever Auraria barber ensured that his name would be well known in the town by taking a cue from Billy the Poet and employing a popular form of advertisement during the 1830s.

"Alexander Scott, Barber and Hair Dresser" . . .
    Informs the friends who on him call
    That he's prepared to shave them all;
    His razors now are very keen,
    The stiffest beard to shave quite clean.
    Soaps, Oils, and Towels, the senses greet,
    They look so fair and smell so sweet.
    His scissors too, make dandies smile,
    They cut the hair in such fine style.
    And Travellers who may visit here,
    Would prosper under Alex's care;
    For 'tis his great and chief delight,
    To make rough faces, a comely sight.
    For all past favors, he now sends,
    His grateful thanks to all his friends;
    And tho' in Latin he's no sponsor,
    Yet signs himself their humble
                  Tonsor[66]

One of the earliest of Auraria's merchants was John Powell, the man credited with suggesting the town's name. Under the corporate name of John M. Powell and Company he offered groceries for a while "at very low prices for Cash only." But the grocery business was apparently not to his liking, and he sold his establishment soon after it opened.[67]

Another well-known merchant during the gold rush was Harrison W. Riley. He was one of the first settlers of Lumpkin County, arriving early in 1833. Although his original intention was apparently to do some gold mining, he quickly decided to leave that dirty work for others. Instead he did his mining indirectly by establishing businesses in which the miners could hand their findings over to him. When Dahlonega was selected as the seat of Lumpkin County, Riley built the town's first store on the east side of the court house square. He later opened a tavern and gambling house. Riley proved to be an opportunist, and by 1838 he was a relatively wealthy man. In the early 1840s he built a large hotel on the town square that for years was the largest one in the area. The

Riley, or Eagle Hotel, as it was also known, was almost half a block long with two large arching doorways and six dormers with arched windows. According to legend, there was once an upstairs bridge that crossed the street between Riley's hotel and his tavern and gambling establishment. Despite his reported participation in several shoot-outs during the 1840s and '50s, Riley lived to serve in the state senate, and in 1861 he was a representative to the secession convention in Milledgeville. By the time of his death in 1874, he was one of the wealthiest men in the state.[68]

Perhaps the most remarkable of the gold region's businessmen was a merchant, miner, and part-time preacher named James Boisclair, or "Free Jim," as he was known to the residents of Dahlonega. At the height of the gold rush, Boisclair arrived in Dahlonega from Augusta and set up a cake and fruit shop. Like other merchants before him, he quickly caught the fever and began to pan for gold. Luck was with him. He discovered a rich vein of gold ore on lot 998 just east of town. He wanted to buy the property, but as a "free person of color" he was not permitted by Georgia law either to buy or sell real estate. Dr. Joseph J. Singleton, the first superintendent of the Dahlonega mint, agreed to serve as Boisclair's guardian, and it was through Singleton that he bought the lot.[69]

Boisclair worked his mine successfully for a decade, making enough money to establish the largest dry goods and general merchandise store in Dahlonega. He also built an ice house, where he stored natural ice during the winter months and sold it throughout the year. Located where the Dahlonega Baptist Church now stands, it was one of the most popular businesses in town. Another popular establishment was Boisclair's saloon—so popular that he was expelled from the Baptist Church of Dahlonega for "selling goods and liquor on Sunday." It is not known what sort of penance he was required to undergo, but he was readmitted to the church about a year later "on recantation."[70] A further problem involving Boisclair's saloon was the difficulty he encountered in obtaining a liquor license. By state law a "free person of color" could not hold such a license. In order to get around the restriction, a white person "for Boisclair" was authorized to sell alcohol at the bar. The license had to be renewed on an annual basis.[71]

Despite relative scarcity and hardship in this frontier region, the Georgia gold country was an exciting place in the 1830s. Wrote one eyewitness of those times, "Scarcely a stream in the whole country but what was thronged with miners, delving after the precious metal, while the hills and valleys were made to reverberate with the busy rattle of machinery, and the clinking of the pick and shovel."[72] At the height of the gold rush there may have been as many as fifteen thousand miners at work in the hills within a ten- or fifteen-mile radius of Dahlonega alone.[73] Many of the miners made their homes in the bark shanties that dotted the mountainous landscape. These dwellings were generally regarded as common property and were occupied by any miner who happened to be digging nearby at the moment.[74]

When the miners were not in the countryside digging for gold, they could usually be found in town looking for ways to spend it. According to one account, "Gambling houses, dancing houses, drinking saloons, houses of ill fame, billiard saloons, and tenpin alleys were open day and night."[75] The men were nearly matched in number by women who were, wrote one citizen of Dahlonega, "equally as vile and wicked."[76] Wrote another eye-witness, "I can hardly conceive of a more unmoral community than exists around these mines; drunkenness, gambling, fighting, lewdness, and every other vice exist here to an awful extent."[77] It appears that as a group the most "moral" people were those denied an opportunity to participate in these festivities—the slaves.[78]

Perhaps the most frequented places of entertainment in the gold region were the drinking saloons. It was these establishments that did the liveliest business in the mining towns, for if the miners did not have enough gold to barter for all their necessities, alcohol was the last thing they forsook.[79] This is not to say that the "houses of ill fame" were any less popular, but with hard liquor selling for less than fifty cents a gallon, whiskey was cheaper than prostitutes.[80] Since coin and currency were less abundant than gold in this frontier region, the going price for a drink was roughly the amount of gold dust that would lie on the point of a knife.[81]

When the Dahlonega miners had too much to drink, they often found themselves "checked in" at a tanyard on the lower end of Water Street known as "Sprawls' Hotel." Being told that it was time to retire, some poor drunken victim would be escorted to Sprawls' by two of his less inebriated companions. There he was led to one of the yard's large open tanning vats and thrown into it. If the man did not immediately come to his senses, he was allowed to "ooze" himself until he was sober enough to check out on his own. According to William P. Price, a printer and news-paper carrier in Dahlonega during the gold rush, no one ever drowned as a result of being registered at Sprawls' Hotel, and the miners seldom allowed themselves more than one visit.[82]

Drunken miners became such a nuisance in Dahlonega that the grand jury felt "compelled to call the attention of our fellow citizens to the increasing number of tippling shops . . . having a most injurious and demoralizing influence upon our community."[83] In Auraria, Agnes Paschal, along with several friends and family members, established a temperance society for which her son, George, was the chief spokesman. Despite the society's efforts to dampen the miners' festivities, drinking saloons remained Auraria's primary attraction during the gold rush. As George Paschal wrote years later in what was surely an understatement, "It will not do to say that [the temperance society] was very prosperous."[84]

Gambling was also a favorite pastime of the miners. Such entertainment as cards, dice, pushpin, horse racing, "chuck-luck" (or "chuck-a-luck"), and even prizefighting attracted hundreds of miners to Dahlonega.[85] According to one town resident, "gambling devices could be seen on the public square both day and night," especially on the weekends.[86] The popularity of gambling drew a horde of "card sharpers" to the gold region, and a good many miners soon discovered that it was easier to lose their gold than to find it. It was not uncommon for a victim to lose the earnings of an entire year in a single night.[87] One eighteen-year-old "greenhorn" who had been practicing with a deck of cards for some time went to town looking for a game and fell into the hands of a professional gambler named Moore. The "sportsman" escorted this young man "down to that den of his, from which no money ever returned, except in the pockets of the gambler," and quickly relieved him of the one dollar and a half with which the youth started.[88] It was fortunate for the poor boy that he did not begin with more.

Arguments over claims of cheating (or any other excuse for a disagreement) would sometimes erupt into free-for-alls. According to one resident of Dahlonega, the din created by these battles "made 'night hideous' with fighting, cursing and swearing."[89] Wrote another Georgian, "Hundreds of combatants were sometimes seen at fisticuffs, swearing, striking and gouging, as frontier men only can do these things."[90] Noisy as they were, these conflicts hardly ever resulted in serious injury, and there is no record of anyone's having died in such a brawl during the gold rush.

Politics provided a less dangerous, if less exciting, diversion for the miners. Residents of the gold region were generally divided into two camps—those who supported the state rights nullification doctrine espoused by Calhoun, and others who favored President Jackson. The dispute between Calhoun and Jackson revolved around the issue of tariffs, among other things.[91] According to Calhoun, individual states, being sovereign within their borders, had the right to ignore, or nullify, acts of the federal government. Following this line of argument, South Carolina chose to nullify the Tariff of 1832. Jackson had no ideological objection to state rights when it came to issues upon which he supported the state's position, as he so clearly demonstrated when he allowed Georgia to nullify the Supreme Court's decision in the *Worcester* case. However, he held no such supportive views with regard to South Carolina's stance.

Many Georgians expressed confusion over how to view Jackson's policy concerning the relationship between the federal and state governments. He had assisted Georgia in its battle with the Supreme Court but now seemed to be a threat to the "rights" of South Carolina. Out of this confusion arose two parties in Georgia, which were largely a reflection of new party alignments developing across the country during Jackson's two terms in office. Though other issues were involved, the party distinctions were based on the question of support for or opposition to Andrew Jackson. The Georgia parties evolved from two state factions that had developed during the previous decade, the Troup Party and the Clark Party. "But now," wrote a resident of Auraria, "the era has arrived when principles, not men are to be maintained in Georgia."[92] Those who had followed former Governor George M. Troup and his Troup Party now termed themselves the State Rights Party and declared their opposition to Jackson's heavy-handed policy toward the states. The adherents of the old Clark Party, named for John Clark, who preceded Troup as governor, formed the new Union Party in support of Jackson. Over the course of the 1830s these Georgia parties merged, albeit incompletely, with their national counterparts. The State Rights faction joined with the Whig Party, and the Unionists gravitated toward the Jacksonian Democrats.[93]

Despite Jackson's previous support of Georgia, many voters felt they owed little to the president. They were of the opinion that Jackson's policy regarding the Indians had been based not on any great respect for the sovereign rights of states, as he revealed in his treatment of South Carolina, but upon his disdain for the Cherokees. Perhaps as a result of Calhoun's influence in Auraria, the *Western Herald* was the voice of state rights in the gold region. One editorial expressed the sentiment that "we do not care what name you call the oppressor. Call him King, or call him President if you please, tis all the same to us, and it is equally immaterial whether his name is George or Andrew. . . . "[94] Emotions on the issue ran so high that another writer in the *Herald* portrayed Jackson as democracy's jailer by asking, "Can the President, with all his omnipotence, bind a man hand and foot, cast him into prison, and whilst in that state, induce him to believe that he is free, and make him boast of his freedom?"[95]

Though Calhoun held considerable sway in Georgia's gold country, it seems that most of the area's residents favored Jackson in spite of his authoritarianism. Dahlonega's first newspaper, the *Miner's Record and Spy in the West*, printed as part of its subheading " . . . devoted to the preservation of the Union and the sovereignty of the States. The sycophant of no party, the slanderer of no individual, the friend of Jackson."[96] Support for Jackson in the gold country was in response primarily to his position on the Cherokees, and it was upon this sentiment that Jackson's backers played. Wrote one ardent Jacksonian, "If we lose Jackson our whole domestic difficulties come down afresh upon us. Away go OUR CHEROKEE LANDS, OUR GOLD MINES to the Indians."[97] If the self-interest of their position was not lost on the good citizens of the gold region, its irony almost certainly was. When election day came, Jacksonian partisans, many of whom were originally from Jackson's home state of Tennessee, carried hickory bushes as symbols of their loyalty to "Old Hickory." Armed with these emblems, they marched to the polls and sent Andrew Jackson back to the White House in 1832 for a second term.[98]

Politics was not the only alternative to drinking saloons and gambling halls as outlets for the miners' emotions. For those so inclined, and there were not many in the gold rush days, religion also provided a source of escape from life's harsh realities. Though demand for spiritual guidance was low, the gold country was not without religious influence. When the gold rush began, there were Christian missionaries ministering to the Cherokees in the area, but because of their opposition to Cherokee removal these men were little loved among the miners, and their services were even less cared for.

It is not surprising that during the height of the gold rush there was minimal concern with spiritual matters among the miners. Their efforts were geared toward acquiring gold rather than salvation. Gold, after all, could be spent; salvation could not. The miners had unwittingly introduced themselves to the historical maxim that the more gold one has, the less God is needed. As a result, the region's first churches were not established until well after the lottery ended in 1833. The Baptists, the largest sect in Georgia, did not have a church in Dahlonega until several years after the town was founded.[99] When Agnes Paschal arrived in Auraria in 1833, there was not a single church of any denomination in the town. She set about organizing one, but the small congregation that resulted from her work had bad luck from the outset.[100] Its first building was a hastily constructed log structure that fell down during the winter of 1833–34.[101] In addition, the small congregation (about a dozen people) was not able to secure a full-time preacher for some time. Conditions for members of Auraria's Antioch Baptist Church became so bad at one point that they disbanded and joined other congregations in the countryside "where they could worship without fear of molestation from the drunken miners, who would often interrupt them during divine service."[102] However, two of the members, "good old Mrs. H." and Agnes Paschal, kept the church going. Before long their plight became known to a Hall County preacher who promised to pay a visit to the church at least once a month, and occasionally a visiting minister would favor the small congregation with a sermon.[103] The First Baptist Church of Canton was more fortunate. Chartered in August 1833 with ten members, it was immediately able to secure the services of Reverend Jeremiah Reeves. Regular pastors, however, were the exception rather than the rule.

Itinerant ministers were occasionally sent into the gold region by various denominations. The Methodist "circuit riders" were particularly diligent in spreading the gospel among the miners.[104] Though most itinerants set out on their missions with the best of intentions, many of them "frequently forgot the sinner, left Satan to his own devices, laid aside their Bibles, and took up the gold pan in pursuit of the yellow mammon, the love of which is reputed to be the root of all evil."[105]

Travel in the gold region was not without its hazards, but it proved particularly dangerous for one circuit rider. It seems there was a blacksmith at Rabun Gap "who had constituted himself its defender against the passage of those pioneers, (the Circuit Riders) of Protestant Christianity; and for 'the vindication of the truth of history.' " Apparently the blacksmith was not in complete agreement with the Methodist interpretation. In any case, it finally became necessary for the Methodists to send "a large burley brother, with a big hard fist" to clear the gap.[106]

Doctors were almost as scarce as ministers in the gold region. There were some in the more populous towns, but few were willing to venture into the rugged countryside at all hours of the day and night. Even worse, a good portion seemed more intent on hunting for gold than practicing their craft on the sick and injured. The task of healing was often left to people like Mrs. William R. King and Agnes Paschal. For many years there was not a single physician in Gilmer County, and Mrs. King was often called upon to perform the functions of both doctor and nurse.[107] Though there were a few doctors in Auraria, the infirm usually preferred the attention of Grandma Paschal. This was largely because of her stern rejection of common medical practices of the day such as leeching, bleeding, and blistering. She relied more on her own philosophy of employing "herbs, ventilated rooms and patient nursing."[108] It comes as no surprise to the modern reader that Grandma's success rate in treating patients was much better than average.

If the gold country could not attract doctors or ministers of the gospel, there was no such difficulty when it came to outlaws. Wrote one Auraria miner in 1833, "I have never before been amongst such a complete sett [sic] of lawless beings. I do really believe, that for a man to be thought honest here, would be a disadvantage to him, or at least he would be set down for a fool and treated accordingly."[109] Gangs of outlaws did roam the area stealing gold and anything else they could get away with, but serious crimes were not as frequent as was widely believed.[110] In Auraria there was only one murder recorded at the height of the gold rush.[111] Most criminal incidents were of a less serious nature, involving such things as horse stealing or other forms of robbery. In writing of the character of the gold region's people, Caroline Gilman expressed surprise at finding that "warm hearts and cultivated minds can live in log cabins and deal in gold."[112]

Nevertheless, in the popular imagination north Georgia remained a wild and lawless country populated by two kinds of people—those who mined gold and those who stole it. But the most famous of the gold robbers was a man who never really existed at all, the murderous outlaw Guy Rivers. William Gilmore Simms visited northern Georgia in the early 1830s collecting background material for his 1834 novel *Guy Rivers: A Tale of Georgia*. Though Simms presented it as a work of fiction, there are those who still believe that the character of Guy Rivers was at least based on a real outlaw who terrorized the antebellum gold region. A local legend has it that he buried his ill-gotten gold in a cave just west of Auraria overlooking the Etowah River. The cave was later part of the Josephine mining property and has been visited by gold hunters ever since the gold rush days. If Guy Rivers or anyone else buried gold in this cave, the treasure remains unknown, at least to the general public.[113]

With outlaws real and imagined in the area, it is no great wonder that the miners sought ways of safeguarding their gold. In the early days of the Intrusion some miners buried their gold or hid it under rocks and in hollow trees. These forms of "banking" had obvious drawbacks, and it quickly became apparent that the miners needed real banks. The Pigeon Roost Mining Company opened Lumpkin County's first bank in Auraria. The company issued notes for use as payment to its employees, and these notes circulated as currency in the county before being presented at the Pigeon Roost office for conversion to gold.[114] Soon regular commercial banks from across the state began to establish branches in the gold region. The Bank of Darien set up offices in Clarkesville, Auraria, and Dahlonega. Clarkesville's own "Farmers Bank of Chattahoochy" also had a branch office in Lumpkin County.[115] These banks helped bring some degree of order to the economic chaos of Georgia's gold country, but the miners needed something more—a local branch of the United States mint where they could have their gold accurately assayed and coined. Their effort to establish a local mint saw its climax in 1838, but this was also a year of disaster, marking a turning point not only for Georgia's gold mining industry but for the Cherokee Nation as well.

Chapter Seven

"Prosper the Americans and Cherokees":
The Climactic Year of 1838

Even with the establishment of banking, trade in the gold region suffered from the lack of a suitable medium of exchange. Only about one coin per person circulated in the area. Credit was difficult to come by. Merchants insisted on immediate payment in cash or gold, and it was they who determined the gold's worth. The gold deposited at banks or bartered to the merchants was in raw, unassayed form, making it difficult to determine its exact value. The bankers, like the merchants, always gave themselves the benefit of the doubt, leaving the miners with little choice but to take what they could get. If the miners disagreed with the assessment of the gold's worth, their options were extremely limited. They could carry their gold to the mint at Philadelphia or to a branch of the Bank of the United States, but that took time. They might also take their gold to a private mint for coining, but after Templeton Reid's Gainesville mint shut down in 1830, the nearest facility was Christopher Bechtler's North Carolina mint. It was obvious to the Georgia miners that what they needed was a local mint. With such a mint, wrote one resident of the gold region, "we shall be enabled to get for the stuff in its native unwrought state the real Jackson shiners themselves."[1]

The suggestion to construct at least one branch mint was made as early as 1831 when the *American Journal of Science and Arts* insisted that such an establishment was needed in North Carolina. So abundant was gold in the South, wrote the *Journal*, that it could be "obtained by slight movements of loose materials, as in some countries are collected at great depths."[2] A proposal for a mint in the Georgia gold region was drawn up at a meeting held at Auraria's Paschal Hotel in November 1833.[3] The idea immediately received the enthusiastic support of John C. Calhoun. Since the senator owned a mine in the area, this could hardly have been a surprise.[4]

The proposal also found favor with Senator Thomas Hart Benton of Missouri, a long-time champion of hard money. His persistent efforts in support of coin over paper currency earned him the nickname "Old Bullion," a distinction in which Benton took great satisfaction. Both he and President Jackson were hard-money advocates and wanted to abolish the Bank of the United States, which, under the direction of Nicholas Biddle, encouraged the type of paper currency and credit system necessary for an expanding economy. Benton endorsed both Jackson's removal of federal deposits from the Bank of the United States and his "specie circular" policy, which stipulated that public lands be paid for in gold or silver.[5]

In 1834 Benton and Representative C. P. White of New York introduced a proposal to increase the value of gold in the United States from a ratio of fifteen to one over silver to a ratio of sixteen to one. They hoped this would encourage the domestic coinage of gold and reduce the transfer of gold to foreign markets where its value was higher.[6] Passage of this legislation, along with the specie circular, resulted in a sharp increase in demand for gold coins that the Philadelphia mint was unable to meet. This situation paved the way for Senator George A. Waggamon of Louisiana to introduce a bill later that year calling for the establishment of branch mints in the South.[7]

Soon after the bill was introduced, a group of Lumpkin County's citizens wrote a letter to Calhoun urging that one of the proposed mints be erected in their county. "It is the most central place in the Gold region," they argued, "about equidistant from the mines of Carroll [County] and Alabama on the South & those of N[orth] Carolina on the North and East, most contiguous to the principal mining operations & to the Chestatee River, which is known of itself to be the richest of all the mines. . . . "[8] Since Calhoun's mine was in Lumpkin County, and near the Chestatee River at that, there was little doubt that he would respond favorably to the suggestion. He ensured that Lumpkin County was specified as the location for the proposed Georgia mint in the final version of the bill.

This Mint Bill sparked lively debate when it was brought before the Senate for consideration. Opposition to the establishment of the branch mints was led by Henry Clay of Kentucky and Theodore Frelinghuysen of New Jersey. Clay was sure that "it would gratify the pride of the States of North Carolina and Georgia to have them there," but felt that these mints would be of little value to the rest of the country.[9] Frelinghuysen wondered why it was necessary to place "an additional burden upon the government because the people in the South have been so fortunate as to find gold?"[10] Supporters of the measure countered with equal zest. Senator Willie Person Mangum of North Carolina objected to Clay's "misconception" regarding the motives of his home state and Georgia. "Those States," he said, "had no pride to gratify."[11] Despite all this political rhetoric, the question at hand in fact revolved around the issue of hard money versus paper currency. Those favoring Jackson and hard money voted for the bill, while supporters of Biddle and the Bank voted against it. The Jacksonians were divided between the "Hards" and "Softs," which almost threw the victory to opponents of the branch mints. But when the final vote was taken, the bill passed by a margin of 24 to 19. It was immediately submitted to the House of Representatives, where on March 3, 1835, it easily won approval. The Mint Act called for the establishment of "one branch at the city of New Orleans for the coinage of gold and silver; one branch at the town of Charlotte [N. C.] . . . for the coinage of gold only; and one branch at or near Dahlonega, in Lumpkin county, in the state of Georgia, also for the coinage of gold only."[12]

Ignatius A. Few was appointed commissioner in charge of establishing the mint at Dahlonega. In August 1835 he selected a site for the building and purchased ten acres just south of town from William J. Worley for $1,050. Few's first choice had been a location on lot 951, adjacent to Dahlonega on the north, but the lot's owner, a Mr. Cassidy of Savannah, refused to sell. The next month Few took bids for construction of the mint. Benjamin Towns of Athens, "a skilful [sic] architect & very respectable, honest man," was the lowest bidder at $33,450. Towns agreed to complete the building within eighteen months, but was allowed a two-month extension in case of "accident, bad weather, or other unavoidable delay."[13]

Though the structure was not completed within the requisite time, Commissioner Few considered it ready for installation of the mint machinery by early 1837. Fifteen large crates containing over fifteen thousand dollars' worth of minting equipment were shipped from Philadelphia to Savannah on April 22. Upon its arrival in Savannah, the massive equipment was transported up river to Augusta, where it was loaded into ten huge wagons for the ten- to fifteen-day overland trip to Dahlonega. The shipment included cutting presses, a fly wheel, a drawing frame, a crank shaft, a coining press, and eighteen annealing pans.[14] In all, the machinery weighed more than twenty-five tons.[15]

Dr. Joseph Singleton, the mint's first superintendent, declared it open for business in February 1838 despite continuing difficulties. The roof leaked, the contractor had not yet vacated the building, the water pump to supply the steam engine would not work, and copper and silver necessary to the coining process had not yet arrived. Nonetheless, gold from the surrounding mines came in so rapidly that almost a thousand ounces were deposited during the first two weeks. It quickly became obvious to Singleton that he could not wait for another shipment from Philadelphia. He borrowed a thousand dollars to buy the needed silver and sent his assistant to Charleston, South Carolina, to get copper for casting the gold into ingots. To power the steam engine, the staff hauled water from a nearby well. Singleton's makeshift efforts proved successful, much to the delight of the local miners. On April 17, more than three years after its construction was approved by Congress, the mint produced its first coins—eighty five-dollar gold pieces.[16]

Depositors from all across the Georgia gold fields made their way to Dahlonega to have their raw gold converted to bullion. The mint also attracted hundreds of visitors anxious to see its fascinating machinery in operation. The most popular piece of equipment was the coining press, which could produce fifty to sixty gold coins per minute.[17] By the end of its first year in operation, the mint produced a total of 20,583 coins with a face value of $102,915.[18]

When the new mint went into operation in 1838, Georgia saw the event as a national affirmation of its policies over the preceding decade toward the Cherokee Nation. This federal establishment in the heart of gold country was a seal of approval and a promise of future prosperity. There was but one task left to be performed which would make the transition to a new age complete—removal of the Cherokees.

Following Georgia's refusal to accept the Supreme Court's decision in the *Worcester* case, accompanied by Jackson's refusal to enforce it, some Cherokees felt that the battle to save their homes was lost. It would be best, they thought, to conclude as favorable a treaty of removal as possible under the circumstances. White intruders were streaming onto Cherokee lands by the thousands, and there seemed to be no way to stop them. Some attorneys for the Cherokees, William Underwood among them, applied for writs of injunction to halt the invasion temporarily pending settlement of titles to individual property. Any judge with the courage to award such writs did so at great personal risk. Judge John H. Hooper, who granted several injunctions, was arraigned for impeachment. The General Assembly further voided his writs by instructing officers of the law charged with their enforcement not to recognize them.[19]

The Assembly also made every effort to encourage the Cherokees to make a treaty with the United States and move beyond the Mississippi. They were making a grave mistake, said the state senate, by continuing to reject the "liberal proposals made by the President. . . . We find the President holding out to them, the most humane and liberal offers, dictated at the same, by the most profound wisdom." Jackson's advocacy of Indian removal was founded "on the most liberal, just and generous policy." According to the senate, such a program served to refute the malicious slander leveled at the United States for its Indian removal policy and proved "the steady perseverance of our government in the path of justice, humanity and virtue."[20] However, as if to demonstrate the limited extent of its own humanity, the General Assembly stipulated that any person who actively discouraged removal among the Cherokees would be fined up to a sum of five hundred dollars or imprisoned.[21]

In spite of attempts to persuade them to leave, most Cherokees clung to the hope that some way might be found to expel the intruders from their land. As it became obvious that their situation was hopeless, some were driven to violence as the only apparent means of combating the intruders. Travel became increasingly hazardous, and it was extremely dangerous for a white person to ride alone after dark. Dr. James Burnes was nearly killed by two assailants who fired at him as they passed on the road just after sunset about three miles from Canton. The bullet passed through the doctor's hat just above his left ear and buried itself halfway in his scalp. "We are glad to say," stated one report, "Dr. B. is not dangerously wounded, though [an] eighth of an inch deeper would have undoubtedly destroyed his life."[22]

In a letter to Governor Lumpkin in 1834, one concerned resident of north Georgia observed that the Cherokees were "more desperate and hostile of late than is usual among them."[23] Another resident confirmed the statement by informing the governor's office that "there is a growing disposition of hostility in the Indians generally. . . ."[24] Much of this Cherokee violence was in retaliation for similar acts on the part of the murderous "Pony Club." The white settlers of Cherokee County became so disturbed at the rising tide of native hostility that they passed a resolution calling for the execution of three Cherokees for every white killed.[25]

The Cherokees' neighbor to the west, the Creek Nation, was having similar troubles of its own. After decades of being squeezed from all sides, the Creeks, once the largest of the Southern nations, were now left with barely two million acres in northeastern Alabama. Even this small remnant was snatched away in 1836 when the U.S. Army moved against the Creeks and forced them westward to "Indian Territory." Hundreds, refusing to go, made a desperate run for Florida in an attempt to join their Seminole cousins. As they drove southeast through Georgia, these refugees clashed with local militia blocking their path all along the way. For a time north Georgians worried that the fighting might spread to the Cherokees, but such fears were unfounded. The great majority of these people had long since rejected violence as an answer to their plight. Chief John Ross denounced fellow Cherokees who participated in attacks on whites even as he continued his own desperate efforts in Washington to avoid a Cherokee Trail of Tears. Still, to many Cherokees it was becoming clear that the choice was simply to fight and die, which most recognized as futile, or to relocate beyond the Mississippi. One Cherokee who stopped by the office of the *Western Herald* to pick up a copy of the paper felt that the only course left to his people was to give up their land to Georgia and move west. With more whites in the Cherokee Nation than natives, it "would be unreasonable," he said of Georgia, "now to stop her and force her to undo what she had done. . . ."[26]

The Cherokees were bitterly divided on the question of westward immigration. The Cherokee Council wrestled with the issue repeatedly, but its delegates were never able to reach an agreement.[27] As a result, the Council broke into two factions: those led by Major Ridge, who saw further strife as futile, and the followers of John Ross, who were determined to continue resistance. Though the removal faction was in the minority, the Council voted to send a delegation headed by John Ridge, son of Major Ridge, to Washington in an attempt to secure a treaty on the best possible terms.

On March 10, 1835, Ridge reported that he had succeeded in negotiating "a treaty made to be sent home for the ratification of the people. It is very liberal in its terms—an equal measure is given to all. The poor Indian enjoys the same rights as the rich—there is no distinction. We are allowed to enjoy our lands in the West."[28] In October the Council met at Red Clay near the present

Georgia-Tennessee border to consider the treaty. Opposition of the Ross faction to removal proved too formidable, and the treaty was rejected. For the sake of Cherokee unity even John Ridge placed his signature on the document of rejection.[29] The government representative, Reverend John F. Schermerhorn, called on the delegates to meet again at New Echota to reconsider the treaty. However, he offered no new terms, and the Council authorized John Ross to return to Washington and resume his efforts to forestall removal.

During Ross's absence all pretence of unity among the Cherokees disintegrated. In December three hundred members of the pro-immigration faction, or "Treaty Party," including Major Ridge, his son John, Elias Boudinot, and Stand Watie, gathered at New Echota to put a removal treaty into final form. During preliminaries to the signing, Major Ridge delivered his position in eloquent and moving terms.

> I am one of the native sons of these wild woods. I have hunted the deer and turkey here more than fifty years. I have fought your battles, have defended your truth and honesty, and fair trading. I have always been the friend of honest white men. The Georgians have shown a grasping spirit lately; they have extended their laws, to which we are unaccustomed, which harass our braves and make the children suffer and cry; but I can do them justice in my heart. . . . I know the Indians have an older title than theirs. We obtained the land from the living God above. They got their title from the British. Yet they are strong and we are weak. We are few, they are many. We cannot remain here in safety and comfort. I know we love the graves of our fathers. . . . We can never forget these homes, I know, but an unbending, iron necessity tells us we must leave them. I would willingly die to preserve them, but any forcible effort to keep them will cost us our lands, our lives and the lives of our children. There is but one path to safety, one road to future existence as a Nation.[30]

Though the futility of further resistance certainly prompted some Cherokees to give in, economic factors were an additional, perhaps even a stronger, motivation. As an inducement to cooperate with the federal government, the lands of those Cherokees who favored removal were exempt from the lottery or secured from confiscation. While other Cherokees such as John Ross and Joseph Vann were evicted from their homes by lottery winners, property belonging to members of the Treaty Party was protected by the state until removal.[31]

On the evening of December 29, 1835, a few delegates of the Treaty Party met in the parlor of Boudinot's house to commence the signing. The making of an unauthorized treaty carried the death sentence by Cherokee law, and Major Ridge prophetically commented as he affixed his mark to the document, "I have signed my death warrant."[32] The Treaty of New Echota called for the Cherokees to relinquish all claims to their eastern lands in exchange for five million dollars and the hollow promise that their new lands in the West would never become part of another state or territory without Cherokee consent.[33]

The vast majority of Cherokees, including Chief John Ross, rejected the Treaty of New Echota and denounced those who signed it as unrepresentative of the official Cherokee position. Nonetheless, the United States government made it clear that if the treaty's terms were not carried out within two years of its signing, federal troops would forcibly evict the Cherokees from their homes.[34]

While the government made preparations to escort the Cherokees west of the Mississippi, efforts to forestall removal continued. Ross and his delegation spent most of 1836 and 1837 in Washington petitioning Congress to reconsider the Indian Removal Act. Wilson Lumpkin, who was elected to the United States Senate in 1837, vigorously resisted any attempts to modify the act or to delay implementation of the Treaty of New Echota. Equally intransigent was George Gilmer, who was returned to the governor's office that same year.[35]

On the other side, such prominent figures as Ralph Waldo Emerson argued just as emphatically for the Cherokee cause. In an open letter to President Martin Van Buren, Emerson warned that if the United States persisted in its efforts to remove the Indians, "the name of this nation, hitherto the sweet omen of religion and liberty, will stink to the world."[36]

Questions of reason and morality notwithstanding, in April 1838 Van Buren ordered Major General Winfield Scott to Georgia with five regiments of regulars and four thousand militia and volunteers. Their mission was to round up the Cherokees and herd them into stockades in preparation for removal. Upon his arrival Scott issued a general call to the Cherokees requesting their compliance in the removal effort. Failure to cooperate, he warned, would result in certain bloodshed. "But spare me," he pleaded, "the horror of witnessing the destruction of the Cherokees." Scott hoped that his message would be "kindly received," and, ignoring his own hypocrisy, closed with a benediction imploring "the God of

It took two men a whole day to fill a boat like this one, but many prospectors thought it worth the effort. A good load might contain as much as forty to fifty dollars' worth of gold. From Phillips, ''Essay on the Georgia Gold Mines,'' 1833.

The better-financed mining companies dug tunnels seven feet square and reinforced them with timbers. However, most miners were far too poor to afford such an investment of money, time, and energy. Their tunnels were no more than four or five feet in diameter and had no timber bracings. The possibility of cave-ins was a constant danger. From Phillips, ''Essay on the Georgia Gold Mines,'' 1833.

Gold-bearing quartz veins were what the miners were after. In this 1934 photo at the Hamilton mine in McDuffie County, mining engineer William H. Fluker points to one of the richest veins of gold ore ever discovered in Georgia. Georgia Department of Archives and History.

Gold ore was most often pushed by miners out of the dark, cramped mines in wooden carts running on wooden tracks. This scene, recorded at the Calhoun Mine at the turn of the century, was typical of Georgia's first and second gold rushes. Georgia Department of Archives and History.

An example of one of the larger stamp mills to operate in nineteenth-century Georgia. After the gold ore was crushed to a near powder, it was washed over a plate lined with "quicksilver," or mercury, to draw out the gold. The gold stuck to the mercury plates and was later separated in a retort vessel. From "Gold Mining in Georgia," *Harper's*, 1879.

More typical of nineteenth-century stamp mills was this small three-stamp structure, photographed in White County in 1895. Georgia Department of Archives and History.

RANAWAY,

FROM the subscriber on the 12th inst. A Negro man by the name of Henry, about eighteen years old, yellow complected, slender made, 5 feet 8 or 10 inches high, has rather a down look, when spoken to, stutters, and materially changes his voice before ending a sentence. He belongs to a gentleman by the name of Eli H. Baxter of Hancock county, Geo. but was in my employ when he absconded in the neighborhood of Auraria, where I have been opperating on a gold mine, and was brought from North Carolina to this state, by a speculator. It is probable that he has been induced to leave, by the persuasion of some white person, Any person apprehending said Negro, and lodging him in any safe Jail, will be suitably rewarded by dropping a line to E. H. Baxter, of Hancock county, or the subscriber in Auraria, Lumpkin county Geo.

NATHAN COOK.

Sept 28 —25—3t,

An announcement of a slave's escape from an Auraria mine. Such notices were common in north Georgia newspapers of the 1830s. From the *Western Herald*, September 28, 1833.

The federal branch mint at Dahlonega. Completed in 1838, it produced more than six million dollars' worth of gold coins before it shut down in 1861. This sketch was made a year after the building was donated to North Georgia College. From the *Mountain Signal*, July 9, 1874.

Shortly after the mint went into operation, the Cherokees were rounded up and forced westward on the Trail of Tears. Nearly one-third died along the way. In later life one old Georgia soldier said, "I fought through the Civil War and have seen men shot to pieces and slaughtered by thousands, but the Cherokee removal was the cruelest work I ever knew." Painting by Marilynn Mallory (1983), Dahlonega Courthouse Gold Museum.

Matthew Stephenson, assayer at the Dahlonega mint. Ironically, the gold began to play out only a few years after Cherokee removal. When word of the new gold strikes in California reached the Georgia miners, hundreds went west. In an unsuccessful effort to keep the miners at home, Stephenson insisted that there was still "gold in them thar hills." Georgia Department of Archives and History.

Nineteenth-century Dahlonega. It was from the steps of the courthouse that Matthew Stephenson urged a group of two hundred miners to remain in Dahlonega rather than head for the newly discovered gold fields of California. Completed in 1836, the building has since 1967 housed the Dahlonega Gold Museum. "Gold Mining in Georgia," *Harper's*, 1879.

Hydraulic mining was brought to Georgia in the 1850s by miners returning from the California gold fields. A single miner using one of these giant water cannons could cut an enormous gash in a mountainside like this one on Crown Mountain just south of Dahlonega. This image was recorded about 1900 at the height of Georgia's short-lived second gold rush. Georgia Department of Archives and History.

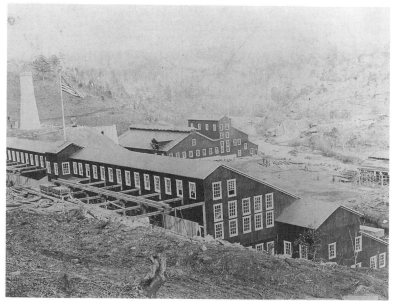

The Dahlonega Consolidated gold plant, the largest ever built east of the Mississippi, was nearly ready to begin operations when this image was recorded in March 1900 at the height of Georgia's second gold rush. Georgia Department of Archives and History.

The huge mill house of the Dahlonega Consolidated sheltered this 120-stamp gold ore crushing mill. Notice the figure seated to the lower left of center. Georgia Department of Archives and History.

Once the thriving center of Georgia's gold region with a population of well over a thousand, Auraria is today a virtual ghost town. Photo by Richard Porter.

The old Graham Hotel is the only structure in Auraria that dates from the gold rush era. It is the last remaining relic of Georgia's first gold rush boom-town. Photo by Richard Porter.

both [to] prosper the Americans and Cherokees, and preserve them long in peace and friendship with each other."[37]

Just before the roundup was to begin, Scott issued orders instructing his troops to render "every possible kindness, compatible with the necessity of removal."[38] Unfortunately for the Cherokees, most of Scott's soldiers were temporary volunteers not used to army discipline, and the general's orders were not always strictly adhered to. A brief account of the scenes that followed were vividly recorded by James Mooney of the Bureau of American Ethnology: "Families at dinner were startled by the sudden gleam of bayonets in the doorway and rose up to be driven by blows and oaths along the weary miles of trail that led to the stockade. Men were seized in their fields or going along the road, women were taken from their [spinning] wheels and children from their play. In many cases, in turning for one last look as they crossed the ridge, they saw their homes in flames, fired by the lawless rabble that followed on the heels of the soldiers to loot and pillage."[39]

Not all Cherokees submitted passively to this treatment. One incident which has become shrouded in legend involved a Cherokee man named Tsali. Details surrounding the sequence of events are still unclear. Some say that Tsali's wife was so brutally treated that he and several other men attempted an escape, and in the ensuing battle a soldier was killed. Other accounts say that a young Cherokee woman was assaulted by a soldier and killed the man with a hatchet. Tsali is said to have hidden the weapon in his shirt and taken responsibility for the murder. Tsali's youngest son, Wasitani, said that his mother was whipped for stopping to care for her baby. Both mother and infant were put on a horse to make better time, but the animal bolted. Tsali's baby was thrown to the ground and killed. According to Wasitani, it was this incident that enraged his people.[40]

In any case, the party made good its escape and fled to the North Carolina mountains. General Scott demanded immediate retribution for the killing. The Cherokees refused and prepared to endure a bloody war against them. At this point, so the legend goes, Tsali struck a bargain with General Scott. He would surrender voluntarily if his people were allowed to remain unmolested in their mountain retreat. Scott agreed, but insisted that three Cherokees must die. As a final useless insult Scott ordered that Tsali be brought in by his Cherokee comrades, and it was they who must perform the executions. On the appointed day Tsali arrived, accompanied by his family and friends. A firing squad was selected from the assembled Cherokees. Tsali, his brother, and his eldest son were killed at the hands of their kinsmen.[41]

Though the legend has gained wide acceptance, it seems to be correct only in part. Tsali and his family apparently did kill perhaps two soldiers, probably as a result of the infant's death, but they did not surrender voluntarily. Instead they were hunted down and executed—not by the Army but by members of another Cherokee family, who in return were allowed to remain in the mountains. Furthermore, another group, the Oconaluftee Cherokees, who lived on land ceded to North Carolina in 1819, were not subject to the Treaty of New Echota. It was these people, not those who killed Tsali, who formed the nucleus of what would later become the Eastern Band of the Cherokees.[42]

By October 1838 most of the Cherokees were in custody, and the long journey to Oklahoma began. The last of the Cherokees left their stockades on November 4.[43] The original plan had been to assemble them at Ross Landing, near the present site of Chattanooga, and travel by water as far as possible. But a severe drought during the summer of 1838 rendered much of the Tennessee River unnavigable. The greater part of the Cherokees would have to make the long winter trek overland.

In late November the rains finally came, followed by snow and bitter cold. The winter of 1838–39 was one of the most extreme on record. Under such conditions there were those who simply could not survive the journey. One witness told of old women who, "apparently nearly ready to drop into the grave, were traveling with heavy burdens attached to the back—on the sometimes frozen ground, and sometimes muddy streets, with no covering for the feet except what nature had given them. . . ."[44] The elderly were the first to die, then the babies, and finally the sick and injured. Each day produced more grief than did the last. One of those who did not complete the journey was Quatie Ross, wife of the chief. She gave up her blanket to a sick child and contracted pneumonia. The child lived, but Quatie never recovered. She died shortly after and was buried near Little Rock, Arkansas.[45]

For some, the emotional wounds of that winter never healed. In later life one old Cherokee remembered how his father collapsed in the snow and died. He was buried by the trail and the family continued on the journey. Then his mother sank down. "She speak no more," he recalled. "We bury her and go on." Finally his five brothers and sisters all became ill and died. "One each day," he said, "and all are gone." Even after the passage of decades, the old man could still hear the cries of his dying family. "People sometimes say I look like I never smile," he said, "never laugh in lifetime."[46]

To rid Georgians of their "Indian problem," the United States government spent almost a million dollars—about sixty-six dollars for each Cherokee.[47] And the expense was measured not only in dollars but in lives as well. Of more than thirteen thousand people who set out on the march, almost five thousand died along the way.[48] Small wonder that this forced migration came to be known as the Trail of Tears. For decades the trail could be traced by following the graves along its route.

Meeting in September 1838, the Lumpkin County grand jury felt compelled to "congratulate our fellow citizens upon the happy event" of Cherokee removal. Members of the jury expressed their thanks to Winfield Scott for expelling "practically the last of the once numerous people from the land of their nativity" and for this extended to him "the honor he so justly merits."[49] In his December message to Congress, President Van Buren echoed the sentiments of the Georgians: "It affords me sincere pleasure to apprise the Congress of the entire removal of the Cherokee Nation of Indians to their new homes west of the Mississippi. The measures authorized by Congress at its last session have had the happiest effects."[50]

Not everyone had such a positive view of the "happy event." After their experience on the Trail of Tears, the Cherokees certainly did not. There were also a good many whites who participated in or witnessed the removal who lamented the treatment of the Cherokees. On reading the president's report, one eyewitness who signed himself "a Native of Maine, traveling in the Western Country" wished that Van Buren could have been in Kentucky on a freezing December day to see the true impact of removal. "When I passed the last detachment of those suffering exiles," he wrote, "and thought that my native countrymen had thus expelled them from their native soil and their much-loved homes, and that too in this inclement season of the year in all their suffering, I turned from the sight with feelings which language cannot express."[51] Z. A. Zile, a Georgia volunteer who took part in driving the Cherokees from their homes and was later a colonel in the Confederate army, also had a perspective of the removal that differed substantially from that of President Van Buren. As an old man reminiscing on the events of his life, he recalled, "I fought through the Civil War and have seen men shot to pieces and slaughtered by thousands, but the Cherokee removal was the cruelest work I ever knew."[52]

"Gold Fever . . . Ain't No Cure For It"

The past is filled with ironies, one of the most profound of which is seen with the climax of the Georgia gold rush. For just as the mint began production and the last of the Cherokees were removed, the reason for both began to disappear, almost as if cursed by the exiled natives. The gold was beginning to play out. Though no one yet knew it, the heyday of the gold rush was over.

By the early 1840s it was becoming increasingly difficult for Southern miners to make a living washing the placer deposits. The mining companies also felt the pressure of diminishing profits.[1] A Nacoochee Valley miner estimated that for every barrel of gold taken from the mines, two barrels' worth was spent in the effort.[2] Area newspapers ran advertisements offering large tracts of land that could "be had on good terms with warranteed good titles."[3] But land that a decade earlier had been worth a gold mine was now difficult to sell. Yet such was the severity of "gold fever" that a good portion of the miners clung to their dreams of quick riches and continued panning the rivers and branches of north Georgia through the rest of the decade. These die-hards were usually able to eke out a meager living, and some even stumbled across rich veins. But such discoveries, said one old miner, "were almost as elusive as the bags of gold that are reputed to lie at the end of the rainbow."[4]

The Dahlonega mint most vividly reflected the declining fortunes of Georgia's gold region in the 1840s. It hit a peak production of nearly six hundred thousand dollars in 1843, but output declined steadily thereafter. By 1849 coinage was less than half what it had been only six years earlier. Though it had produced almost one and a half million gold coins with a face value of over six million dollars by the time it shut down in 1861, the mint fulfilled neither national nor local expectations. Its production was never enough to help overcome the national shortage of coins, as had been hoped. It did not even smooth out the local economy, since gold coins did not freely circulate in the area. They were considered much too valuable for that.[5] As Senator Henry Clay of Kentucky had predicted, the Dahlonega mint held out a promise to Georgia and the nation which could never be realized.[6] Some hint of things to come might also have been taken from George W. Featherstonhough, who traveled through the gold region in the summer of 1837. Even before the mint opened, he felt that this imposing structure looked somehow out of place in Dahlonega. In his words, it gave the little mountain town "an air of pretension."[7]

As early as 1841 there was a determined effort in Congress to discontinue the Dahlonega mint, and a proposal to shut it down was doggedly pushed by some congressmen for the next twenty years.[8] But the facility was kept in operation despite increasing opposition in Congress. Though it cost much more to operate than was warranted by its declining annual production, the mint was a politically popular institution.[9] It provided jobs for Dahlonega residents, and, despite protests to the contrary, its presence indeed served to gratify the pride of Georgia.[10]

By 1849 word of the great California strikes had reached the gold-hungry miners of Georgia, and they began making ready for the long journey westward. Dr. Matthew Stephenson, amateur geologist and assayer at the Dahlonega mint, called a meeting at the town square to discuss the matter. Mounting the courthouse steps to address a crowd of around 200 miners, Stephenson chastised them for allowing their heads to be turned by fantasies of gold in California. Waving his hand toward Findley Ridge, just south of Dahlonega on Crown Mountain, the good doctor shouted, "Why go to California? In that ridge lies more gold than man ever dreamt of. There's millions in it."[11]

Despite Stephenson's admonitions, the miners left for California in droves—so many that one nineteenth-century mining engineer called the Southern gold region "the cradle (in fact, literally the *rocker*), in which the California '49-er was born."[12] Hundreds of miners like Lewis Ralston, a longtime resident of the gold region and friend of Benjamin Parks, abandoned their mountain homes.[13] Even William Reese Crisson, one of the original Georgia twenty-niners, joined the exodus to California.[14]

Though the miners did not take Stephenson's advice, they took his parting phrase with them. "There's millions in it" became a well-known saying among the California forty-niners, and it kept them digging there even if it did not inspire hope among the old twenty-niners on Findley Ridge. This phrase, which Mark Twain later attributed to the character of Mulberry Sellers, gave rise to the more widely known cry "Thar's gold in them thar hills."[15] But in the Georgia gold fields, said one old-timer, "the gum rockers, [long] toms, sluices, and pounding mills were left to rot in the gulches and on the river banks, and the ditches were turned over to the tender mercies of the industrious crawfish."[16]

James Boisclair, like so many others, was caught up by the wave of California gold fever and left Dahlonega to pursue his fortune in California. In 1850 he contracted with about fifty men to pay their way to the new Western *El Dorado* in exchange for half their first year's earnings. Such an arrangement might have doubled or tripled his already substantial wealth, but it was not to be. When Boisclair arrived in California, he found not fortune but fate. Somehow he became involved in an argument over a claim. The quarrel turned violent and Boisclair, age forty-six, was shot to death. But his memory lives on in the Georgia gold country, where the mine he worked for ten years is still known as "The Free Jim."[17]

More fortunate than James Boisclair were Dan and Lucinda Riley of Cherokee County, a free black couple who farmed and panned for gold on the side. Though they did not strike it rich in California, they at least made a few thousand dollars and lived to return home. However, as the story goes, it was only chance that made it possible for them to try their luck in California. Like other Georgia miners, Dan and Lucinda caught gold fever in 1849 and yearned to go west, but they were much too poor to make the journey—for the moment. Shortly after hearing of the California gold strike, Dan hit a rich vein of gold while panning along a stream adjacent to the property of Jacob Scudder, his former master. At a certain point along the stream, Dan noticed that the gold was "coarse and ragged," indicating the presence of a nearby vein. He traced the gold to its source on a hill bordering the stream, dug down about three feet, and hit a rich quartz vein. Dan scooped up a pan of dirt from the top of the vein, panned it out, and found so much gold that, as he later said, "it looked like [I] had dug into a yellow jacket's nest."[18] His first thought was that now he and Lucinda could go to California. His second was to keep his find a secret. While digging, he noticed a few of Scudder's slaves working in the distance on the other side of the stream and was afraid that they might have seen him. He quickly filled in the hole and erased all trace of his work. The next day Dan sold his findings for seventy dollars, and he and Lucinda were on their way to California.

In their later years, after the California gold played out, they returned to Georgia with the intention of locating the rich vein

Dan had discovered so long ago. They searched the area for years, digging holes all along the stream, but could never find the old vein. Dan told his story to Richard Carnes, a local farmer and part-time miner who often helped the old couple in their searches. Even after Dan and Lucinda passed away, Carnes continued to look for the mine—to no avail. The tale has been passed down for over a century, and to this day folks in Cherokee County still enjoy telling the story of the "Lost Negro Mine."[19]

The 1850s saw a renewed interest in Georgia gold with the advent of hydraulic mining. This process, developed in California, involved the construction of canals to transport water from high mountain streams to the mines. The water, pulled down by gravity, was funneled into a giant hose, and the elevation of the canals provided enough force to wash tons of dirt from the mountains. Several hydraulic mining companies were formed, and by the end of the decade great gashes were being cut in the Georgia hillsides. Another new process often used in conjunction with hydraulic mining was blast mining. Tunnels and shafts were dug, and the ore was blasted loose with dynamite or kegs of gunpowder. Then the giant hydraulic hoses were used to wash it out. One of the largest operations of this type was the Canton Mining Works in Cherokee County. It had a network of shafts and tunnels running hundreds of feet across and two hundred feet down.[20]

Despite advancements in mining, Georgia's "forgotten industry" continued its decline through the end of the decade. A contributing factor was another exodus to the West with the discovery of gold in Colorado. Three brothers from Auraria, W. Green, Levi J., and J. Oliver Russell, led a party of miners to the banks of Cherry Creek and founded a new settlement. They called it Auraria in remembrance of their Georgia home. In 1860 Auraria, Colorado, merged with another fledgling settlement on the opposite bank to become the town of Denver.[21]

The coming of the Civil War delivered the final blow to gold mining as a major industry in Georgia. The mint closed in 1861, and mining in the area came to a virtual standstill.[22] The Dahlonega mint was never reopened. After the war the building housed federal troops, who occupied Dahlonega until 1869. Later that year the Treasury Department decided to sell the old building. The highest offer was only $1,525, and the government did not accept it. In 1871 Representative William P. Price of Dahlonega persuaded his colleagues in Congress to transfer title of the property to the trustees of North Georgia Agricultural College, which opened its doors two years later. In 1879 the main building caught fire and burned to the ground. Nothing was left but the foundation and the stone walls of the basement. Another structure was built in its place, and today, still standing on the basement walls of the old mint, Price Memorial Hall serves as the administration building for North Georgia College. In commemoration of the college's 100th anniversary, the steeple of Price Memorial was leafed with thirteen ounces of gold from the surrounding hills.

Mining continued sporadically after the war, and a few hydraulic operations were set up. Some new companies were even established. One of the largest was the Hand Gold Mining Company. Backed mainly by investors from Cleveland, Ohio, the Hand Company erected stamp mills and built miles of pipelines to support hydraulic mining in the 1870s.[23] But really significant interest in large-scale gold mining was not seen again until the turn of the century, when the development of new mining technology sparked a second Southern gold rush.

Between 1899 and 1901 several companies set up gold-processing plants in the vicinity of Dahlonega. In June 1899 the most ambitious of these, the Dahlonega Consolidated Gold Mining Company, began construction of a 120-stamp mill on the banks of Yahoola Creek just east of town. The main building measured 300 by 100 feet and was four stories tall, making it the largest gold plant ever built east of the Mississippi River.[24] This period also saw a revival of dredge mining. One of the largest of the dredge boats was owned by the Bunker Hill Mining Company. During the first years of the twentieth century, it brought tons of gold-bearing gravel up from the bottom of the Chestatee River.[25]

Despite huge capital investments and a gold production of $62,000 in 1903 and almost $100,000 the next year, the new gold mining companies could not turn a profit.[26] The once vaunted Dahlonega Consolidated, chartered at half a million dollars in capital stock, shut down in 1903 and was auctioned off three years later for $20,000.[27] The giant complex, in the words of one witness, now stood "as a whited sepulcher over departed hopes and promises."[28] The other large mining facilities soon followed suit, bringing to an end Georgia's second gold rush.[29]

Gold fever again swept Georgia briefly in the 1930s in the wake of the Great Depression. Several mines were briefly worked, including the Hamilton in McDuffie County; the Franklin in Cherokee County; the Thompson in White County; and the Lockhart, Battle Branch, and Pigeon Roost (Barlow) in Lumpkin County. But these proved to be no more productive than the mines of thirty years earlier. The same held true for the venture of Graham Dugas, who in 1939 reopened the old Calhoun Mine. He made a good deal of money persuading investors to finance the scheme, but the mine itself produced little wealth.[30]

There is not much left of the old mines and milling plants that held such promise for generations of Georgia miners. A few holes in the hillsides are virtually all that remain. Most of the machinery was sold in the late 1930s to Japanese buyers who came through the area looking for scrap iron. Since then there have been no serious attempts to mine Georgia gold on a large scale, but folks in the gold region are still stricken with that curious disease known as gold fever. Amy Trammell came to Auraria in 1925 and "caught the gold fever. And there ain't no cure for it. No, that's been a long, long time now and I've got it just as bad as I had it back then." Marion Boatfield, who grew up panning gold around Dahlonega, says of gold prospectors, "Just tell me one that ever quit it as long as he could stay at it."[31]

Expressions of that spirit are visible all across north Georgia: in the old Lumpkin County Courthouse, built in 1836, which today houses the Dahlonega Gold Museum; in the thirteen ounces of gold that cover the steeple of Price Memorial Hall; in the forty-three ounces of gold on the dome of Georgia's state capitol. And that spirit is recaptured every October during the Gold Rush Days festival, when Dahlonega is thronged by would-be prospectors reliving the antebellum gold mining days during which thousands of twenty-niners poured into the area and swept away the Cherokees.

Though the Cherokees lived in the southern Appalachians for generations, it took only a decade to dislodge them from their mountain homes. The state of Georgia made them "tenants at will"; the gold rush brought thousands of intruders down upon them; the lottery gambled away their inheritance; and Andrew Jackson, in ignoring his Constitutional obligation, sealed their fate. By 1839 the once mighty Cherokee Nation had been driven westward on the Trail of Tears. Though the Cherokees are gone, their legacy remains. Place names such as Nacoochee, Chestatee, Etowah, and Dahlonega serve constantly to remind Georgians that their ancestors were not the first to settle this land.

The Georgia gold rush is now more than a century and a half past, but some folks believe the gold is still there in abundance. Says Marion Boatfield, "There's still plenty of gold around here, and there always will be." But she is quick to add that "what's left is deep and hard to get at."[32] John Crisson, a modern gold miner and descendant of generations of gold miners, agrees. "All the free gold has played out. . . . It would take a million-and-a-half dollars to get a successful operation going today. A number of folks have tried to do it with less and have gone broke." Perhaps it takes folks with mining in their blood to know that, as Crisson says, "there are no short cuts to gold mining."[33] Nevertheless, the Crisson Mine has met with some success since its opening in 1970, as has the Dahlonega Condolidated, which reopened in 1991. And geologists have recently confirmed that veins rich in gold do indeed lie undisturbed in these Appalachian foothills. A few have even predicted that another really big strike may yet be made.[34] Of course this comes as no surprise to the old-timers. They've been saying that for years.

Notes

INTRODUCTION

1. The transition from a hunter-gatherer existence (Paleolithic) to an agricultural village life-style (Neolithic) began almost simultaneously in several different areas of the world such as the eastern Mediterranean, Mesoamerica, India, and China. This occurred as a result of population pressures and climatic changes following the last ice age, about twelve thousand years ago.

2. Jenifer Marx, *The Magic of Gold*, 5.

3. The mountains of the British Isles and Scandinavia were once part of this range but broke from North America as the continents began to split more than 250 million years ago. See C. F. Park, Jr., "Gold Deposits of Georgia," 107; George F. Becker, "Reconnaissance of the Gold Fields of the Southern Appalachians," 252. For a geologic overview of the gold belt see Jerry German, "The Geology of the Northeastern Portion of the Dahlonega Gold Belt."

4. C. S. Anderson, "Gold Mining in Georgia," 62.

5. For overviews of gold mining in the South, see Otis E. Young, Jr., "The Southern Gold Rush, 1828–1836"; Nancy Roberts, *The Gold Seekers*; Robert A. Russell, "Gold Mining in Alabama Before 1860"; Fletcher M. Green, "Georgia's Forgotten Industry: Gold Mining," "Gold Mining: A Forgotten Industry of Ante-Bellum North Carolina," and "Gold Mining in Ante-Bellum Virginia"; "Gold in Maryland" (*American Journal of Science and Arts*).

6. Ulrich B. Phillips, *Georgia and State Rights*, 35.

7. W. R. Crandall, "The Hydraulic Elevator at the Chestatee Mine, Georgia," 62.

8. *Mountain Signal*, August 18, 1882.

CHAPTER ONE—

"No Talke, No Hope, Nor Worke, But Dig Gold":
The Origins of Southern Gold Fever

1. *Atlanta Constitution*, July 15, 1894; *Dahlonega Signal*, November 17, 1893. A partial reproduction of the *Constitution* article can be found in Andrew W. Cain, *History of Lumpkin County for the First Hundred Years, 1832–1932*, 93–94.

2. Brian M. Fagan, *The Great Journey: The Peopling of Ancient America*, 132–34.

3. George F. Becker, "Gold Fields of the Southern Appalachians," 253; W. S. Yeates, S. W. McCallie, and Francis P. King, "A Preliminary Report on a Part of the Gold Deposits of Georgia," 26.

4. Yeates, McCallie, and King, 26.

5. Becker, 253.

6. Frederick W. Hodge, "The Narrative of Alvar Núñez Cabeza de Vaca," 21–22; Becker, 253–54; Yeates, McCallie, and King, 26. The natives may also have been referring to copper since it too was mined in the southern Appalachians. See Sharon I. Goad, "Copper and the Southeastern Indians," 50–54.

7. Theodore H. Lewis, "The Narrative of the Expedition of Hernando de Soto, by the Gentleman of Elvas," in *Spanish Exploration in the Southern United States, 1528–1543,*154, 164.

8. De Soto's route remains a matter of controversy. Some writers place it as far north as Kentucky, though most think this unlikely. For information on de Soto's route through Georgia and the South see George H. Heye, F. W. Hodge, and George H. Pepper, *The Nacoochee Mound in Georgia*, 5–6, 7; Marvin T. Smith, "The Route of De Soto Through Tennessee, Georgia, and Alabama: The Evidence from Material Culture"; John R. Swanton, "Final Report of the United States De Soto Expedition Commission," xxiii–xxix.

9. Charles C. Jones, Jr., *The History of Georgia*, 58; Yeates, McCallie, and King, 28.

10. Becker, 254–56.

11. C. C. Jones, 58; Becker, 256. In his 1935 article, Fletcher M. Green cites as evidence of Spanish gold workings a village unearthed in Nacoochee Valley in 1834 which was then several hundred years old ("Georgia's Forgotten Industry: Gold Mining," 97). The news article on which Green based this assumption describes houses made of notched logs from six to ten inches in diameter, and the article's author speaks of pottery of which "the high finish and its exact dimensions induce me to believe it the production of a more civilized people than the present race of Indians" (*Southern Banner*, June 21, 1834). However, more recent excavations reveal that Indians of the Southeast indeed built such structures and manufactured pottery of "high finish" and "exact dimensions."

12. Thomas G. Clemson, "Gold and the Gold Region," 62–63.

13. Fletcher M. Green, "Gold Mining in Ante-Bellum Virginia," 228–29.

14. F. M. Green, "Gold Mining: A Forgotten Industry of Ante-Bellum North Carolina," 5.

15. F. M. Green, "Gold Mining in Ante-Bellum Virginia," 231.
16. F. M. Green, "Gold Mining: A Forgotten Industry of Ante-Bellum North Carolina," 6.
17. Clemson, 62.
18. Ibid.
19. J. Hector St. John de Crèvecoeur, *Letters from an American Farmer* (1793) in F. M. Green, "Gold Mining: A Forgotten Industry of Ante-Bellum North Carolina," 6–7.
20. Otis E. Young, Jr., "The Southern Gold Rush," 375–76; Linda Funk, "The Reed Gold Mine," 2–3; Bruce Roberts, *The Carolina Gold Rush*, 7–8. See also Richard F. Knapp, "Golden Promise in the Piedmont: The Story of John Reed's Mine."
21. J. T. Pardee and C. F. Park, "Gold Deposits of the Southern Piedmont," 31.
22. Denison Olmsted, "On the Gold Mines of North Carolina," 15.
23. Charles E. Rothe, "Remarks on the Gold Mines of North Carolina," 215–16.
24. Pardee and Park, 31.
25. The *Norfolk Herald*, in the *Cherokee Phoenix*, August 12, 1829.
26. James Mooney, "Myths of the Cherokee," 116.
27. W. H. Fluker, "Gold Mining in McDuffie County, Georgia," 119.
28. Lucian Lamar Knight, *A Standard History of Georgia and Georgians*, 366–67.
29. Ibid.
30. W. Larry Otwell, *The Gold of White County, Georgia*, 5.
31. Ulrich B. Phillips, *Georgia and State Rights*, 35.
32. For a map of Cherokee and Creek land cessions in Georgia see Mrs. J. E. Hays, "Indian Treaties and Cessions of Land, 1705–1837." See also Charles C. Royce, "The Cherokee Nation of Indians."
33. U.S. Commissioners to Creek Chiefs, December 9, 1824, in "American State Papers, Indian Affairs," II, 570.
34. Edward J. Harden, *The Life of George M. Troup*, 206. For an examination of the status of Indians in Georgia see Mary Young, "Racism in Red and Black."
35. Kenneth Coleman, *A History of Georgia*, 130; Thurman Wilkins, *Cherokee Tragedy*, 164–65; Michael D. Green, *Politics of Indian Removal*, 96.
36. Coleman, 130–31; George W. Paschal, *Ninety-Four Years: Agnes Paschal*, 218.

37. William G. McLoughlin, "Compulsory Indian Removal," 608.

38. For a brief overview of the state of Cherokee civilization on the eve of the controversy with Georgia see William C. Sturtevant, "John Ridge on Cherokee Civilization in 1826." See also Douglas C. Wilms, "Cherokee Land Use in the State of Georgia 1800–1838."

39. McLoughlin, 608.

40. The Cherokees were much more interested in the schools than they were in the churches. In 1826 about 5 percent were Christian, and by 1835 that figure had risen to approximately 9 percent. Theda Perdue, *Cherokee Editor: The Writings of Elias Boudinot*, 80, n. 9 & 10. Most Cherokees practiced the traditional Cherokee religion, of which the nineteenth-century anthropologist James Mooney wrote: "So far from being a jumble of crudities, there is a wonderful completeness about the whole system which is not surpassed even by the ceremonial religions of the East. It is evident . . . that the Cherokee Indian was a polytheist and that the spirit world was to him only a shadowy counterpart of this. All his prayers were for temporal and tangible blessings—for health, for long life, for success in the chase, in fishing, in war and in love, for good crops, for protection and for revenge. He had no Great Spirit, no happy hunting ground, no heaven, no hell, and consequently death had for him no terrors and he awaited the inevitable end with no anxiety as to the future." See Mooney, "Sacred Formulas of the Cherokees," 319.

41. By 1835 two hundred and nine Cherokee heads of families were slaveholders, accounting for 7.5 percent of all family heads. However, no more than twenty can be called planters (defined as those who owned 20 or more slaves). Only three owned more than 50. Among the more prominent Cherokee slaveholders were John Ross (19 slaves), John Ridge (21 slaves), Major Ridge (15 slaves). Joseph Vann headed the list with 110 slaves. See R. Halliburton, Jr., *Red Over Black: Black Slavery Among the Cherokee Indians*, 181–92. See also Theda Perdue, *Slavery and the Evolution of Cherokee Society.*

42. Perdue, *Cherokee Editor: The Writings of Elias Boudinot*, 72.

43. George R. Gilmer, *First Settlers of Upper Georgia*, 246–47.

44. Sturtevant, 88.

45. "Acts of the General Assembly of the State of Georgia, 1826," 208.

46. "Journal of the Senate of the State of Georgia, 1827," 215, 223.

47. Ibid., 221.

48. McLoughlin, 610–11.

49. Thomas McKenney to Thomas Stuart, April 14, 1828, in ibid., 618.

50. McLoughlin, 611–25.

51. "Journal of the House of Representatives of the State of Georgia, 1828," 186.

52. "Acts of the General Assembly of the State of Georgia, 1828," 88–89.

53. Ibid.

54. Gilmer, 247.

CHAPTER TWO—
"Acting Like Crazy Men":
Gold Fever and the Great Intrusion

1. See H. David Williams, "Origins of the North Georgia Gold Rush."

2. W. S. Yeates, S. W. McCallie, and Francis P. King, "A Preliminary Report on a Part of the Gold Deposits of Georgia," 33.

3. Fletcher M. Green, "Georgia's Forgotten Industry: Gold Mining," 99.

4. *Mountain Signal*, July 16, 1874.

5. S. P. Jones, "Second Report on the Gold Deposits of Georgia," 183; "Memories of Dahlonega" by W. R. Crisson in the *Dahlonega Signal*, April 13, 1894. Crisson's "Memories of Dahlonega" were published in a series of articles appearing in the *Dahlonega Signal* during the spring and summer of 1894. Portions are loosely transcribed in Andrew W. Cain, *History of Lumpkin County*, 74–78. The Pigeon Roost claim is found on page 74.

6. Lucian Lamar Knight, A scrapbook of newspaper clippings on Georgia history, 18: 142.

7. William P. Blake, "Report Upon the Property of the Mining Company Called the Auraria Mines of Georgia," 5; *Mountain Signal*, July 16, 1874; Yeates, McCallie, and King, 29.

8. Jacob Peck, "Geological and Mineralogical Account of the Mining Districts in the State of Georgia–Western Part of North Carolina and of East Tennessee," 3.

9. Georgia newspapers mention discoveries of gold in the Carolinas, Virginia, and even Vermont between 1826 and 1828 but say nothing of gold in Georgia until the summer of 1829. See the

Southern Recorder, September 5, 1826, September 12, 1826, August 13, 1827, February 25, 1828, August 9, 1828; and the *Georgia Journal,* August 1, 1829.

10. Sherry Boatright, "The Calhoun Gold Mine," a–11.

11. Yeates, McCallie, and King, 271.

12. Larry E. Mitchell, "Benjamin Parks: A Really Golden Heritage," 23. The Parks family Bible housed at the Dahlonega Courthouse Gold Museum gives Benjamin Parks's birth date as October 27, 1802.

13. Lucian Lamar Knight, *Georgia's Landmarks, Memorials and Legends,* 846.

14. *Atlanta Constitution,* July 15, 1894; Mitchell, 23.

15. *Atlanta Constitution,* July 15, 1894.

16. O'Barr sold the property to Joseph Rucker, William White, Lemuel Banks, and William H. Underwood on January 9, 1830. Three years later, on June 25, 1833, John C. Calhoun bought the mine for six thousand dollars. See Boatright, a–11.

17. *Atlanta Constitution,* July 15, 1894.

18. Samuel Moore, Director, U.S. Mint, to John C. Calhoun, December 20, 1833, in Clyde N. Wilson, *Papers of John C. Calhoun,* 12: 194. A year later Calhoun commented that the mine was not doing as well as he had originally anticipated (ibid., 371). It was not until September 1835 that he expressed optimism about the mine's future (ibid., 555).

19. *Georgia Journal,* August 1, 1829.

20. *Macon Telegraph,* September 17, 1831.

21. *Niles' Register,* June 5, 1830. Though the term "miner" evokes the image of a person working a tunnel or shaft, it may be used to describe any individual engaged in the extraction or panning of minerals, whether deep within the earth or on its surface.

22. F. M. Green, "Georgia's Forgotten Industry," 101; George R. Gilmer, *Sketches of Some of the First Settlers of Upper Georgia, of the Cherokees, and the Author,* 264.

23. *Atlanta Constitution,* July 15, 1894.

24. F. M. Green, "Goergia's Forgotten Industry," 100.

25. *Mountain Signal,* July 16, 1874; William P. Blake and Charles T. Jackson, "Gold Placers in the Vicinity of Dahlonega, Georgia," 6.

26. F. M. Green, "Georgia's Forgotten Industry," 100.

27. Gilmer, 265.

28. Major Phillip Wager to Major General Alexander Macomb, September 30, 1830, in James W. Covington, "Letters from the Georgia Gold Region," 407–8.

29. F. M. Green, "Georgia's Forgotten Industry," 101.

30. "Memories of Dahlonega" by W. R. Crisson in the *Dahlonega Signal*, April 20, 1894.

31. "Memories of Dahlonega" by W. R. Crisson in the *Dahlonega Signal*, April 13, 1894.

32. *Southern Recorder*, October 3, 1829.

33. Caroline Gilman, *Poetry of Travelling in the United States*, 293.

34. *Georgia Journal*, August 1, 1829.

35. Many of these reports told of gold finds in the counties of Hall and Habersham (the western part of which was later made White County). However, much of this gold was actually being mined illegally within the bounds of the Cherokee Nation in what would become Lumpkin County.

36. *Southern Recorder*, October 3, 1829.

37. *Southern Recorder*, November 14, 1829.

38. *Southern Recorder*, March 27, 1830. The price of gold in the 1830s was close to twenty dollars an ounce.

39. *Southern Recorder*, September 25, 1830.

40. *Southern Recorder*, February 6 and April 17, 1830; *Niles' Register*, June 5, 1830.

41. *Cherokee Phoenix*, quoted in the *Southern Recorder*, June 28, 1832.

42. *Niles' Register*, June 5, 1830.

43. C. P. Gordon to Col. Hamilton Brown, November 1, 1830, in T. Conn Bryan, "Letters Concerning Georgia Gold Mines," 339; quote from William L. Gwyn to Col. Hamilton Brown, January 31, 1833, in ibid., 343.

44. *Southern Recorder*, November 14, 1829.

45. *Southern Recorder*, July 3, 1830.

46. Yeates, McCallie, and King, 36.

47. *Southern Recorder*, October 2, 1830.

48. Not to be confused with the Pine Mountain located sixty miles to the south in Harris County.

49. Yeates, McCallie, and King, 242.

50. Adiel Sherwood, *A Gazetteer of the State of Georgia*, 87; "Statistics of Coinage" (*Hunt's Merchants' Magazine*), 384.

51. As late as the turn of the century it was one of the two periods from which the mountain folk dated all events, "the other being 'the late [Civil] war.' " See "Gold Mining in Georgia," 509–10.

52. "Acts of the General Assembly of the State of Georgia, 1828," 89.

53. *Cherokee Phoenix*, February 11, 1829. From 1828 to 1835 the *Cherokee Phoenix* was the mouthpiece of the Cherokee Nation, and it remains the best source on the conflict from the Cherokee point of view. A complete file is on microfilm at the Georgia Department of Archives and History in Atlanta.

54. *Cherokee Phoenix*, February 25, 1829.

55. *Cherokee Phoenix*, May 27, 1829.

56. *Cherokee Phoenix*, February 4, 1829.

57. *Atlanta Constitution*, July 15, 1894.

58. *North Carolina Spectator*, April 30, 1830; *Southern Recorder*, April 10, 1830.

59. F. M. Green, "Georgia's Forgotten Industry," 102.

60. Gilmer, 266–67.

61. Ibid., 268.

62. Ibid., 267–69.

63. Ibid., 267.

64. Ibid., 278.

65. *Georgia Journal*, August 1, 1829.

66. *Southern Recorder*, April 24, 1830.

67. *Southern Recorder*, November 13, 1830.

68. Gilmer, 278.

69. Ibid., 265; *Southern Recorder*, September 4, 1830.

70. *Columbus Enquirer*, quoted in *Niles' Register*, October 9, 1830; *Southern Recorder*, October 2, 1830.

71. *Niles' Register*, October 9, 1830.

72. "Memories of Dahlonega" by W. R. Crisson in the *Dahlonega Signal*, June 29, 1894.

73. Ibid.; *Mountain Signal*, July 16, 1874.

74. Major Phillip Wager to General Alexander Macomb, September 15 and 20, 1830, in Otis E. Young, Jr., "The Southern Gold Rush, 1828–1836," 385.

75. *Cherokee Phoenix*, September 6, 1832.

76. Ibid.

77. Lieutenant Abram C. Fowler to Major Wager, September 26, 1830, in Covington, 408–9.

78. B. L. Goodman to George Gilmer, June 7, 1830, in Covington, 403.

79. Gilmer to President Andrew Jackson, June 17, 1830, in Covington, 404–7.

80. *Niles' Register*, October 30, 1830.

81. Cherokees to Commander of the U. S. troops, October 4, 1830, in Cain, 33.

82. *Niles' Register*, April 23, 1831.
83. *Cherokee Phoenix*, March 26, 1831.
84. *Cherokee Phoenix*, January 21, 1832.
85. Ibid.
86. *Southern Recorder*, September 25, 1830.
87. "Acts of the General Assembly of the State of Georgia, 1830," 154–56.
88. "Acts of the General Assembly of the State of Georgia, 1830," 114–17, 155.
89. *Georgia Journal*, January 27, 1831; Colonel John W. Sanford to Governor Gilmer, January 22, 1831, in *Niles' Register*, March 12, 1831. A portion of this letter is reproduced in Cain, 34. Another account of the Battle of Leather's Ford can be found in Gilmer, 297–301.

CHAPTER THREE—
"Get a Little Further":
The Cherokee Nation Abandoned

1. *Niles' Register*, June 13, 1829.
2. Ross to Crockett, January 13, 1831, in Gary E. Moulton, *John Ross: Cherokee Chief*, 42.
3. David Crockett, *A Narrative of the Life of David Crockett of the State of Tennessee*, 206.
4. Crockett to A. M. Hughes, February 13, 1830, in James A. Shackford, *David Crockett: The Man and the Legend*, 118–19.
5. Crockett, 206.
6. Robert V. Remini, *Andrew Jackson and the Course of American Freedom, 1822–1832*, 259–60.
7. For a detailed treatment of Wilson Lumpkin's role in Cherokee removal both as a congressman and later as governor of Georgia, see Carl J. Vipperman, "Wilson Lumpkin and the Cherokee Removal."
8. Remini, 260.
9. Wilson Lumpkin, *Removal of the Cherokee Indians from Georgia, 1822–1832*, 1: 83.
10. Henry Clay to Jeremiah Evarts, August 23, 1830, in Francis Paul Prucha, *Cherokee Removal: The "William Penn" Essays and Other Writings by Jeremiah Everts*, 30.
11. Remini, 161, 163.
12. Shackford, 212.
13. Thurman Wilkins, *Cherokee Tragedy: The Ridge Family and the Decimation of a People*, 214.

14. John Hutchins, "The Trial of Reverend Samuel A. Worcester," 364.

15. Wirt to Gilmer, June 4, 1830, in *Niles' Register*, September 18, 1830. A more complete overview of Wirt's arguments was published in *Niles' Register*, September 25, 1830, under the title "The Cherokee Case."

16. Gilmer to Wirt, June 19, 1830, in *Niles' Register*, September 18, 1830.

17. Hutchins, 364.

18. *Niles' Register*, January 8, 1831.

19. Ibid. In later years William Underwood lived near the Alabama border and sometimes crossed the state line to practice law. On one occasion he was reminded by a certain young upstart attorney that Georgia law held no sway in Alabama. In reply Underwood recalled his experience with case of Corn Tassels: "My young friend has reminded me that I could not introduce Georgia law into his state. . . . I will let him understand that of which he seems to be ignorant, to wit: that Georgia takes the liberty of extending her laws over all the adjacent savage tribes, and, what concerns the young man personally still more, with very little evidence or ceremony she hangs or sends to the penitentiary all the young savages that traduce her, or are in any manner in her way." The Southern Historical Association, *Memoirs of Georgia*, 2: 280.

20. Register of Debates in Congress, VII (1831), 715–16, in Wilkins, 220.

21. *Cherokee Phoenix*, March 26, 1831.

22. *Cherokee Phoenix*, April 16, 1831.

23. "Acts of the General Assembly of the State of Georgia," 1830, 114–17.

24. Wilkins, 225.

25. "Acts of the General Assembly of the State of Georgia, 1830," 116.

26. Ulrich B. Phillips, *Georgia and State Rights*, 79.

27. Hutchins, 370–73.

28. *Niles' Register*, March 17, 1832.

29. Moulton, 46.

30. *Niles' Register*, September 13, 1830.

31. Boudinot to Stand Watie, March 7, 1832, in Wilkins, 235.

32. This remark was originally attributed to Jackson by Horace Greeley in his work *The American Conflict* (1866). Though it is unlikely that Jackson uttered this exact phrase, there can be little doubt that it accurately reflected his attitude.

33. Wilkins, 236.

34. *Cherokee Phoenix,* July 20, 1833.

35. Worcester and Butler to Charles J. Jenkins, Attorney General of the state of Georgia, January 8, 1833, in *Niles' Register,* February 2, 1833.

36. *Niles' Register,* February 2, 1833.

37. *Niles' Register,* June 20, 1829.

38. George W. Paschal, *Ninety-Four Years: Agnes Paschal,* 227–28.

CHAPTER FOUR—
"Civilized Life" Comes to the Gold Region

1. For a discussion of the lottery's impact on the Cherokees see H. David Williams, "Gambling Away the Inheritance."

2. George G. Ward, *The Annals of Upper Georgia,* 54; "Acts of the General Assembly of the State of Georgia, 1830," 127–31.

3. Joel Dixon Wells, *Sixth or 1832 Land Lottery,* iv.; "Acts of the General Assembly of the State of Georgia, 1830," 127–28; "Acts of the General Assembly of the State of Georgia, 1831," 164.

4. Douglas C. Wilms, "Georgia's Land Lottery of 1832," 54. For a complete overview of the Georgia lotteries see Robert Scott Davis, Jr., and Silas Emmet Lucas, *The Georgia Land Lottery Papers, 1805–1914.*

5. George R. Gilmer, *First Settlers of Upper Georgia,* 285.

6. Ibid., 284–85.

7. Wilson Lumpkin, *Removal of the Cherokee Indians from Georgia, 1827–1838,* 1: 128.

8. *Macon Advertiser,* September 23, 1831.

9. *Macon Telegraph,* September 17, 1831. Gilmer's popularity also suffered because of his efforts to grant Cherokees the right to testify against whites in courts of law. This was no reflection of any affinity Gilmer had for the Cherokees but an attempt to make it easier to prosecute the gold diggers. But many, like the editor of the *Macon Telegraph,* accused Gilmer of being "extremely anxious to place the ignorant and vindictive savage upon the same footing with the free white citizen." *Macon Telegraph,* September 3, 1831.

10. *Cherokee Phoenix,* December 24, 1831. For a list of those persons who won gold lands see M. D. J. Slade, *Prizes Drawn in the Cherokee Gold Lottery.*

11. George W. Paschal, *Ninety-Four Years: Agnes Paschal,* 230–31. As it happened, none of the Paschal tickets were matched with a gold or land lot.

12. Joel Chandler Harris, *Stories of Georgia*, 216.

13. *Western Herald*, December 14, 1833. The *Western Herald*, Auraria's newspaper for less than a year between 1833 and 1834, was unknown to scholars for over a century until the discovery of a complete file in the early 1950s. It was this file that became the basis for E. Merton Coulter's *Auraria: The Story of a Georgia Gold-Mining Town*. Though published for only a short time, the *Western Herald* remains the most detailed source of information for, as Coulter put it, "a close-up view of an exciting period of gold-mining history in the South" (Coulter, *Auraria*, ix). A complete copy of the *Western Herald* file is on microfilm at the University of Georgia library.

14. "Acts of the General Assembly of the State of Georgia, 1830," 131–34.

15. "Acts of the General Assembly of the State of Georgia, 1831," 164–67.

16. "Acts of the General Assembly of the State of Georgia, 1830," 134–35.

17. "Acts of the General Assembly of the State of Georgia, 1830," 134–35; *Niles' Register*, February 19, 1831.

18. *Georgian*, October 4. 1832; James F. Smith, *Cherokee Land Lottery*, vii.

19. *Niles' Register*, November 24, 1832.

20. *Western Herald*, December 14, 1833.

21. *Niles' Register*, October 27, 1832.

22. "Acts of the General Assembly of the State of Georgia, 1832," 24–25.

23. *Georgian*, October 4, 1832.

24. "Georgia Surveyor General Department," 14–15; Wells, iv.

25. E. Merton Coulter, "Reminiscences of Benjamin Franklin Matthews," 198–200.

26. Cherokee County Historical Society, *Glimpses of Cherokee County*, 23–24; Lloyd G. Marlin, *History of Cherokee County*, 147. A near verbatim reproduction of Marlin's story of Mary Franklin can be found in Roy E. Bottoms, "History of the Franklin Gold Mine," 3–4.

27. It was on these lots that the Dahlonega Consolidated Gold Mining Company set up the largest gold mining plant ever to exist east of the Mississippi River. It conducted operations from 1900 to 1903.

28. "Gold Mining in Georgia" (in *Harper's New Monthly Magazine*), 510.

29. "Dahlonega, or Georgia Gold Region," 113; *Southern Recorder*, May 1, 1833.

30. Paschal, 236–37.

31. Mary Bondurant Warren, *Alphabetical Index to Georgia's 1832 Gold Lottery*, xiii–xv.

32. Ibid., xiii; "Acts of the General Assembly of the State of Georgia, 1834," 160–61.

33. *Niles' Register*, December 15, 1832.

34. "Acts of the General Assembly of the State of Georgia, 1830," 141–42.

35. "Acts of the General Assembly of the State of Georgia, 1832," 102.

36. "Acts of the General Assembly of the State of Georgia, 1834," 159.

37. *Cherokee Phoenix*, November 24, 1832.

38. *Macon Advertiser*, June 21, 1831.

39. "Acts of the General Assembly of the State of Georgia, 1831," 74.

40. Sandra W. Payne, "Historic Tour of Pickens County."

41. The town of Tate remained part of Cherokee County until 1853, when it was absorbed by the newly created Pickens County. "Acts of the General Assembly of the State of Georgia, 1831," 74–75; "An Historical Sketch of Pickens County" (Works Projects Administration Project); Cherokee County Historical Society, *Glimpses of Cherokee County*, 11; Lucius Eugene Tate, *History of Pickens County*, 44–45.

42. "Acts of the General Assembly of the State of Georgia, 1832," 56. Cass County was renamed Bartow in 1861. All these counties have since been partitioned to form additional counties.

43. *Niles' Register*, May 4, 1833.

44. "Acts of the General Assembly of the State of Georgia, 1832," 58.

45. Andrew W. Cain, *History of Lumpkin County*, 42.

46. *Niles' Register*, May 4, 1833. A nearly complete reprint of the article can be found in Cain, 43–44.

47. *Georgia Messenger*, April 25, 1833.

48. Ibid.; George Raffalovich, "Dead Towns of Georgia." It is difficult to say with any certainty how many people actually lived in Lumpkin County in 1833. Many of the county's inhabitants composed a transient population of miners. While it is possible that there were as many as ten thousand people working the Lumpkin

County mines, the Georgia state census of 1834 gives a resident population of 5,272.

49. *Western Herald,* April 9, 1833.

50. The General Assembly organized the county in December 1832 and named it after the governor, Wilson Lumpkin.

51. *Western Herald,* April 9, 1833; Coulter, *Auriaria,* 8–9.

52. Cain, 42–43.

53. Ibid., 43.

54. The Inferior Court was roughly equivalent to what is to-day referred to as Probate Court.

55. Doris Bray Kenimer, *Gold in Them Thar Hills,* 18; Cain, 61; Paschal, 234–35.

56. As it happened, the case was not settled until February 1836. Plummer's grant was canceled and the lot divided equally between the state and the informer, Nathaniel Nuckolls. See court records in Cain, 61–62.

57. *Western Herald,* April 30, 1833.

58. Ibid.

59. *Western Herald,* June 25, 1833.

60. *Western Herald,* July 16, 1833.

61. *Western Herald,* July 9, 1833.

62. *Southern Banner,* August 3, 1833; *Western Herald,* July 23, 1833.

63. *Western Herald,* September 7, 1833; Cain, 62.

64. *Memoirs of Georgia,* 2: 470; William P. Blake and Charles T. Jackson, "Gold Placers in the Vicinity of Dahlonega," 10–11; *Dahlonega Signal,* November 17, 1893.

65. *Niles' Register,* October 26, 1833; James Mooney, "Myths of the Cherokee," 514.

66. William P. Blake, "Prospectus of the Chestatee Hydraulic Company," 16; *Mountain Signal,* August 27, 1880; George White, *Historical Collections of Georgia,* 542.

67. *Niles' Register,* October 26, 1833; Cain, 63.

68. "Acts of the General Assembly of the State of Georgia, 1833," 334.

69. *Western Herald,* November 30, 1833.

70. *Georgian,* March 29 and June 27, 1834.

71. Cain, 63.

72. *Niles' Register,* October 26, 1833.

73. Fletcher M. Green, "Georgia's Forgotten Industry: Gold Mining," 109.

74. In 1856 the western half of Habersham and part of eastern Lumpkin County became White County.

75. Victor Bristol, "History of Early Settlers of Nacoochee Valley," 66. See also White County Centennial Committee, *Historical Facts and Legends of White County: 1857–1957.*

76. *Southern Recorder,* April 17 and July 3, 1830.

77. *Southern Banner,* August 3, 1833.

78. *Southern Recorder,* July 3, 1830.

79. *Southern Recorder,* August 3, 1833.

80. *Southern Banner,* June 1, 1833.

81. *Macon Advertiser,* June 21, 1833.

82. Caroline Gilman, *Poetry of Travelling in the United States,* 288.

83. *Macon Advertiser,* June 21, 1833.

84. F. M. Green, "Georgia's Forgotten Industry," 111.

85. *Southern Recorder,* October 2, 1830.

86. *Southern Banner,* June 1, 1833.

87. Cherokee County Historical Society, *Glimpses of Cherokee County,* 27.

88. "Acts of the General Assembly of the State of Georgia, 1832," 58.

89. Marlin, 46.

90. *Glimpses of Cherokee County,* 27.

91. Marlin, 46.

92. *Southern Banner,* June 1, 1833; George White, *Statistics of Georgia,* 178.

93. S. W. McCallie, "The Gold Deposits of Georgia," 173.

94. *North Carolina Spectator,* July 30, 1830; W. S. Yeates, S. W. McCallie, and Francis P. King, "Gold Deposits of Georgia," 242.

95. *Southern Banner,* June 1, 1833.

96. Ibid.

CHAPTER FIVE—

"It's Just Like Gambling—All Luck":
Mining in the Gold Rush Days

1. William P. Blake and Charles T. Jackson, "Gold Placers in the Vicinity of Dahlonega," 6.

2. *Atlanta Constitution,* July 15, 1894.

3. William Phillips, "Essay on the Georgia Gold Mines," 2–5; W. Larry Otwell, *Panning Georgia's Gold,* 56; William P. Blake, "Prospectus of the Chestatee Hydraulic Company," 12.

4. W. Phillips, 1–2.

5. Ibid., 14. A complete description of the panning process can be found in Otwell, *Panning Georgia's Gold,* 16–20.

6. *Dahlonega Nugget*, January 29, 1897. The *Dahlonega Nugget* saw its first printing in 1890 but did not begin uninterrupted publication until 1897, when W. B. Townsend became editor. The weekly paper has been in existence ever since. See Austin F. Dean, *Observations from a Peak in Lumpkin*.

7. *Dahlonega Nugget*, January 29, 1897; W. Phillips, 14; T. Conn Bryan, "The Gold Rush in Georgia," *Georgia Review*, 398; "Gold Mining in Georgia" (*Harper's New Monthly Magazine*), 508–9; Otis E. Young, Jr., "The Southern Gold Rush," 387.

8. W. Phillips, 15.

9. Ibid., 15–16.

10. *Dahlonega Nugget*, January 29, 1897.

11. "Gold Mines of North Carolina" (*American Journal of Science and Arts*), 363.

12. D. Reinhardt to Denison Olmsted, June 4, 1829, in "Gold Mines of North Carolina," 362–63.

13. *Georgia Journal*, March 10, 1831.

14. "Gold Region of the United States" (*American Journal of Science and the Arts*), 349.

15. *Western Herald*, June 11, 1833.

16. W. Phillips, 17.

17. Blake, "Prospectus," 19.

18. *Western Herald*, April 9, 1833.

19. *Western Herald*, May 21, 1833.

20. Blake, "Prospectus," 20.

21. Fletcher M. Green, "Georgia's Forgotten Industry: Gold Mining," 217.

22. Reinhardt to Olmstead, June 4, 1829, in "Gold Mines of North Carolina," 363.

23. Charles E. Rothe, "Remarks on the Gold Mines of North Carolina," 215–16; Jacob Peck, "Mining Districts in the State of Georgia," 4.

24. William M. Brewer, "Further Notes on the Alabama and Georgia Gold Fields," 406; S. W. McCallie, "A Preliminary Report on the Mineral Resources of Georgia," 95–96.

25. W. Phillips, 12–13.

26. *Southern Banner*, December 28, 1833; Caroline Gilman, *Poetry of Travelling in the United States*, 292; W. S. Yeates, S. W. McCallie, and Francis P. King, "Gold Deposits of Georgia," 174; Blake and Jackson, 8.

27. "Gold Region of the United States," 350.

28. Yeates, McCallie, and King, 218.

29. *Southern Banner,* December 28, 1833.
30. George White, *Statistics of the State of Georgia,* 393.
31. C. S. Anderson, "Gold Mining in Georgia," 63.
32. White, *Statistics,* 303. The deepest mine in Georgia appears to have been the Creighton Mine, formerly the Franklin. At the turn of the century its shafts reportedly ran 500 feet below the surface (C. S. Anderson, 63).
33. "Gold Region of the United States," 350.
34. W. Phillips, 13.
35. O. E. Young, 379.
36. Garland Peyton, "The Old-Time Stamp Mill," 93.
37. *Dahlonega Nugget,* January 29, 1897.
38. White, *Statistics,* 393.
39. W. H. Fluker, "Gold Mining in McDuffie County," 121.
40. Peyton, *Statistics of the State of Georgia,* 94. A small stamp mill can be viewed at the Gold Museum in Dahlonega, Georgia. A larger version can still be seen in operation at the Crisson Mine where Cavender Creek Road intersects with U.S. 19 two miles north of Dahlonega.
41. White, *Statistics,* 393; Peyton, 94–95; Ben Cooper, *Dahlonega Gold,* 24; Lou Harshaw, *The Gold of Dahlonega,* 34.
42. Georgia-Alabama Investment and Development Co., "Prospectus of the City of Tallapoosa," 11.
43. Wilber Colvin, "Gold Mining in Georgia," 10.
44. Charles Lanman, *Adventures in the Wilds of the United States and British American Provinces,* 1: 348–49.
45. Yeates, McCallie, and King, 174, 199.
46. George B. Ward, *Annals of Upper Georgia, Centered in Gilmer County,* 105; S. P. Jones, "Second Report on the Gold Deposits of Georgia," 270.
47. S. W. McCallie, "The Gold Deposits of Georgia," 173.
48. *Southern Recorder,* October 2, 1830.
49. *Southern Banner,* December 28, 1833.
50. White, *Statistics,* 303.
51. Sherry Boatright, "The Calhoun Gold Mine," a–11.
52. John C. Calhoun to James Edward Calhoun, September 23, 1835, in Clyde N. Wilson, *The Papers of John C. Calhoun,* 12: 555.
53. *Western Herald,* April 9, 1833.
54. *Western Herald,* August 24, 1833; *Niles' Register,* September 14, 1833.
55. *Western Herald,* November 30, 1833.

56. John C. Calhoun to James Edward Calhoun, September 23, 1835, in Wilson, 12: 555.

57. *Western Herald*, November 30, 1833.

58. *Western Herald*, October 19, 1833.

59. *Southern Banner*, August 3, 1833.

60. "Acts of the General Assembly of the State of Georgia, 1832," 88–94.

61. "Acts of the General Assembly of the State of Georgia, 1832," 89–94; "Acts of the General Assembly of the State of Georgia, 1834," 128–31; "Acts of the General Assembly of the State of Georgia, 1837," 130–31; "Mineral Wealth of Georgia" (*Hunt's Merchants' Magazine*), 632.

62. "Acts of the General Assembly of the State of Georgia, 1834," 128–31.

63. F. M. Green, "Georgia's Forgotten Industry," 218.

64. *Niles' Register*, April 7, 1832.

65. *Macon Advertiser*, May 24, 1831.

66. F. M. Green, "Georgia's Forgotten Industry," 218.

67. *Georgian*, May 3, 1834.

68. "Acts of the General Assembly of the State of Georgia, 1834," 143; *Georgian*, January 12, 1835.

69. *Western Herald*, November 2, 1833.

70. Yeates, McCallie, and King, 466.

71. *Federal Union*, November 22, 1832.

72. *Western Herald*, September 7, 1833. Other examples of such notices can be found in the *Georgia Journal*, May 9 and 16, 1833.

73. *Southern Banner*, December 28, 1833.

74. *Western Herald*, November 2, 1833.

75. *Southern Recorder*, April 24, 1830.

76. F. M. Green, "Georgia's Forgotten Industry," 214.

77. From a pamphlet on mining published by W. R. Crisson, August 1, 1875, part of which is contained in Andrew W. Cain, *History of Lumpkin County for the First Hundred Years, 1832–1932*, 113.

78. George F. Becker, "Gold Fields of the Southern Appalachians," 258; Blake, "Prospectus," 12.

79. Blake, "Prospectus," 13.

80. *Dahlonega Nugget*, January 29, 1897.

81. *Southern Recorder*, October 3, 1829.

82. Thomas G. Clemson, "Gold and the Gold Region," 60.

83. *Dahlonega Signal*, April 20, 1883; "Memories of Dahlonega" by W. R. Crisson in the *Dahlonega Signal*, April 13, 1894; *Dahlonega Nugget*, January 29, 1897. Bernal Díaz, who accompa-

nied Hernando Cortez on his conquest of New Spain, noted that the Mexican Indians carried quills filled with gold (Díaz, *The Conquest of New Spain*, 233).

84. "Reminiscences of Miss Fanny Wood," in Cain, 53.

85. Blake and Jackson, 8.

86. *Georgia Journal*, October 22, 1834; *Southern Banner*, February 8, 1834.

87. F. M. Green, "Georgia's Forgotten Industry," 220; A. S. Furcron, "Gold Production in Georgia," 24.

88. Nicholas Biddle to John C. Calhoun, September 11, 1833, in Wilson, 12: 171–72.

89. *Southern Recorder*, July 24, 1830.

90. F. M. Green, "Gold Mining: A Forgotten Industry of Ante-Bellum North Carolina," 139–40; F. M. Green, "Georgia's Forgotten Industry," 220; O. E. Young, 382. Green gives the spelling as "Betchler," but Young and contemporary sources show the spelling as "Bechtler" (*North Carolina Spectator*, July 2, 1831; *Georgia Courier*, October 3, 1831).

91. *Southern Recorder*, July 24, 1830.

92. Ibid.

93. *Georgia Courier*, August 16, 1830. According to the letter, Reid's ten-dollar gold pieces were worth $9.38, the five-dollar pieces were worth $4.69, and the two-and-a-half-dollar pieces were worth $2.35.

94. *Georgia Journal*, September 11, 1830; Dexter C. Seymour, "Templeton Reid, First of the Pioneer Coiners," 244, n. 70.

95. "Georgia Gold," *American Journal of Science and Arts*, 255–56.

96. Seymour, 237.

97. *Atlanta Constitution*, August 30, 1987.

98. Seymour, 244.

99. L. W. Richardson, "Templeton Reid: Early Georgia Coin Maker," 38.

100. Ibid., 31.

CHAPTER SIX—

"Gambling Houses, Dancing Houses, & Drinking Saloons":
Life in the Georgia Gold Region

1. *Dahlonega Nugget*, January 29, 1897.

2. William P. Blake, "Prospectus of the Chestatee Hydraulic Company," 16.

3. "Mining Interest at the South" (*Russell's Magazine*), 442.

4. See H. David Williams, "Georgia's Forgotten Miners: African-Americans and the Georgia Gold Rush." Fletcher M. Green included some mention of black miners in "Georgia's Forgotten Industry: Gold Mining," but only briefly. Certainly the dearth of material was a factor. Even now it is difficult to make definite pronouncements or come to firm conclusions on Georgia's black miners. Documentation is fragmentary at best, and much of the evidence is little more than oral tradition. For information on slaves and gold mining in other states of the antebellum South see F.M. Green, "Gold Mining: A Forgotten Industry in Antebellum North Carolina," 12, 15, and "Gold Mining in Antebellum Virginia," 361–63; Edward W. Phifer, "Jr., Champagne at Brindletown: The Story of the Burke County Gold Rush, 1829–1833." See also John C. Inscoe, *Mountain Masters, Slavery, and the Sectional Crisis in Western North Carolina*, 72–79 passim; Robert S. Starobin, *Industrial Slavery in the Old South*, 23–24, 214–19; Brent D. Glass, "Midas and Old Rip: The Gold Hill Mining District of North Carolina," 133–43.

5. William P. Blake and Charles T. Jackson, "Gold Placers in the Vicinity of Dahlonega," 7; *Georgia Journal*, December 14, 1833.

6. O. E. Young, 381–82.

7. *State Rights' Sentinel*, February 16, 1836.

8. E. Merton Coulter, *George Walton Williams*, 11–12.

9. O. E. Young, 381.

10. "Reminiscences of Miss Fanny Wood," in Andrew W. Cain, *History of Lumpkin County for the First Hundred Years, 1832–1932*, 53.

11. F. M. Green, "Georgia's Forgotten Industry," 218.

12. John C. Calhoun to James Edward Calhoun, September 23, 1835, in Clyde N. Wilson, *The Papers of John C. Calhoun*, 12: 555.

13. *Western Herald*, January 31, 1834.

14. *Western Herald*, April 9, 1833.

15. *Niles' Register*, August 7, 1830.

16. George C. Ward, *Annals of Upper Georgia Centered in Gilmer County*, 105.

17. Minutes of the Superior Court of Lumpkin County, August 22, 1833.

18. Mary L. Church, *The Hills of Habersham*, 11.

19. Forest C. Wade, *Cry of the Eagle*, 79.

20. Roy E. Bottoms, "History of the Franklin Gold Mine," 4; Lloyd G. Marlin, *History of Cherokee County*, 147.

21. Caroline Gilman, *Poetry of Travelling in the United States*, 294.

22. *Western Herald*, September 21, 1833. This description of slave mannerisms is revealing in that it shows them as typical of the way slaves were encouraged to behave. African Americans, whether slave or free, learned early in life to assume a posture of submission when being spoken to by any white person. For a slave to speak back in a quick or lively manner was considered "uppity," and violation of this slave society etiquette resulted in severe punishment. Alcohol served as a temporary, if infrequent, escape from the slave's harsh existence. See Kenneth M. Stampp, *The Peculiar Institution*, 145–46.

23. *Western Herald*, September 28, 1833.

24. *Western Herald*, October 26, 1833.

25. *Southern Banner*, April 13, 1833.

26. Kenneth Coleman, *A History of Georgia*, 185.

27. Wade, 79.

28. George W. Paschal, *Ninety-Four Years: Agnes Paschal*, 277.

29. *Dahlonega Signal*, August 6, 1886. Even today there are few African Americans living in what was Georgia's antebellum gold region. They constitute less than 10 percent of the population in Georgia north of Fulton County. Thomas W. Hodler and Howard A. Schretter, *Atlas of Georgia*, 201.

30. *Western Herald*, August 10, 1833.

31. Ward, 105.

32. Ibid.

33. F. M. Green, "Georgia's Forgotten Industry," 211.

34. "Dahlonega, or Georgia Gold Region" (*Hunt's Merchants' Magazine*), 113.

35. *Southern Banner*, May 18, 1833.

36. Ibid.

37. William P. Blake, "Report Upon the Property of the Mining Company Called the Auraria Mines of Georgia," 5.

38. *North Carolina Spectator*, May 21, 1830.

39. W. S. Yeates, S. W. McCallie, and Francis P. King, "Gold Deposits of Georgia," 475–77; Cain, 111–12. See also C. F. Parks and R. A. Wilson, *The Battle Branch Gold Mine*.

40. William Gilmore Simms, *Guy Rivers: A Tale of Georgia*, 13–14, 15.

41. William L. Gwyn to Col. Hamilton Brown, December 23, 1833, in T. Conn Bryan, "Letters Concerning Georgia Gold Mines," 346.

42. Gilman, 287–88.

43. *Southern Banner*, May 25, 1833.

44. Ibid.

45. *Mountain Signal*, January 30, 1875.

46. For a short overview of Agnes Paschal and the Paschal family see H. David Williams, "Agnes Paschal: The Angel of Auraria"; and Sybil McRay, "Paschal Family Tree." For a more detailed treatment see Paschal.

47. *Western Herald*, April 9, 1833.

48. *Western Herald*, June 11, 1833.

49. Williams, "Agnes Paschal," 82.

50. *Western Herald*, April 9, 1833.

51. *Western Herald*, October 26, 1833.

52. *State Rights' Sentinel*, August 21, 1834.

53. Lucius Eugene Tate, *History of Pickens County*, 34; Robert S. Davis, "Indians of Pickens County," 37; E. Merton Coulter, *Auraria: The Story of a Gold-Mining Town*, 21.

54. "Reminiscences of William A. Hutcheson," in Cain, 54; *Dahlonega Nugget*, January 29, 1897.

55. "Reminiscences of William Hutcheson," in Cain, 54.

56. *Dahlonega Nugget*, January 29, 1897.

57. *Western Herald*, April 9, 1833.

58. Ibid.

59. *Western Herald*, August 24, 1833.

60. *Western Herald*, April 16, 1833.

61. *Western Herald*, April 23, 1833.

62. *Western Herald*, June 11, 1833.

63. Ibid.

64. Ibid.

65. Ibid.

66. *Western Herald*, April 16, 1833.

67. *Western Herald*, June 11, 1833.

68. *Mountain Signal*, November 7, 1874; Census of Georgia, Lumpkin County, 1838; Cain, 336–38; Jimmy E. Anderson, "The Life and Troubled Times of General Harrison W. Riley," 33–36.

69. W. P. Price, *Sixty Years of the Life of a Country Village Baptist Church*, 18; Yeates, McCallie, and King, 439.

70. Price, 18; Yeates, McCallie, and King, 439; *Dahlonega Nugget*, June 1, 1917.

71. Liquor Selling Licenses, Court of Ordinary, Lumpkin County, Georgia, Georgia Department of Archives and History.

72. *Mountain Signal*, January 30, 1875.

73. From a letter written by R. H. Gordon, July 4, 1881, in Cain, 101.

74. *Dahlonega Nugget*, January 29, 1897.

75. Price, 44.

76. Ibid.

77. "Georgia Gold," Georgia Department of Natural Resources.

78. O. E. Young, 380.

79. Blake and Jackson, 10. As late as 1880, one Georgia editor wrote, "Gold is found in thirty-six counties in this State, silver in three, copper in thirteen, iron in forty-three, diamonds in twenty-six, and whiskey in all of them, and the last gets away with all the rest." (*National Labor Tribune*, December 18, 1880).

80. Frank L. Owsley, *Plain Folk of the Old South*, 116.

81. *Dahlonega Signal*, April 20, 1883.

82. Price, 44.

83. Report of the Lumpkin County Grand Jury, August 1835, in Cain, 66.

84. Paschal, 247.

85. George R. Gilmer, *First Settlers of Upper Georgia*, 265; *Western Herald*, April 30, 1833; Price, 19, 44–45.

86. Price, 19, 44.

87. *Dahlonega Nugget*, January 29, 1897.

88. Garnett Andrews, *Reminiscences of an Old Georgia Lawyer*, 73–74.

89. Price, 44.

90. Gilmer, 265.

91. A tariff is a tax placed on imported goods which forces the distributor to raise prices to make up for the loss, in turn forcing consumer costs up and making it easier for domestic manufactures to compete.

92. *Western Herald*, December 21, 1833.

93. The national party designations were not used for state elections in Georgia until the early 1840s. Prior to that time, state officials ran either as Unionists or State Righters. See Kenneth A. Coleman, *A History of Georgia*, 411, n. 4.

94. *Western Herald*, November 16, 1833.

95. *Western Herald*, December 21, 1833.

96. Cain, 325.

97. *Federal Union*, August 23, 1832.

98. Paschal, 238.

99. See Price.

100. See Minutes of the Antioch Baptist Church in Auraria.

101. Cain, 47.

102. Paschal, 314.

103. Ibid.

104. Lloyd G. Marlin, *History of Cherokee County*, 171; Cain, 209.

105. Cain, 47.

106. Andrews, 92.

107. Ward, 96.

108. Paschal, 26.

109. William L. Gwyn to Col. Hamilton Brown, January 31, 1833, in Bryan, "Letters Concerning Georgia Gold Mines," 343.

110. F. M. Green, "Georgia's Forgotten Industry," 210.

111. "Reminiscences of Miss Fanny Wood," in Cain, 53; Coulter, *Auraria*, 47–48.

112. Gilman, 289.

113. Andrew Sparks, "Is $3,000,000 Buried in a Georgia Cave?" *Atlanta Journal and Constitution Magazine*, August 16, 1953, 20–22.

114. Cain, 413; Paschal, 271. A photograph of an original Pigeon Roost note can be found in Cain, 52.

115. *Federal Union*, April 30 and May 7, 1834; *Southern Banner*, February 8, 1834; Cain, 415.

CHAPTER SEVEN—
"Prosper the Americans and Cherokees":
The Climactic Year of 1838

1. *Georgian*, February 11, 1835. "Jackson shiners" referred to the gold coins that would be produced by a federal branch mint in Georgia's gold region.

2. "Miscellanies" (*American Journal of Science and the Arts*).

3. George W. Paschal, *Ninety-Four Years: Agnes Paschal*, 272; *Western Herald*, November 23, 1833.

4. *State Rights' Sentinel*, May 15, 1835; Clyde N. Wilson, *Papers of John C. Calhoun*, 12: 501.

5. Louis S. Sears, "Thomas Hart Benton," 211; Thomas Hart Benton, *Thirty Years' View*, 1: 436–58. A complete discussion of the bank controversy can be found in George Rogers Taylor, *Jackson vs. Biddle's Bank*.

6. A. Barton Hepburn, *History of Coinage and Currency in the United States*, 38–41.

7. Sylvia Gailey Head and Elizabeth W. Etheridge, *The Neighborhood Mint*, 15. The severe depletion of the money supply also led to an economic depression two years later known as the Panic of 1837. When Martin Van Buren became president in March of

that year, there were already indications of a downturn in the economy. The unemployed had recently rioted in Northern cities, and in the South cotton was less than half its normal price. In May, banks across the country suspended withdrawals of silver and gold. It was hoped that the new Southern branch mints would pump enough coin into circulation to ease the situation, but their production proved much too limited for that. So disastrous was the panic that a contemporary, presaging the sentiments of a later depression-era generation, wrote years afterward, "It is . . . impossible for those of the present generation to comprehend the effects, moral and social, of such a financial crisis as occurred in 1837." (Paschal, 275).

8. Henry M. Clay (a citizen of Lumpkin County, not the congressman from Kentucky), et al., to John C. Calhoun, January 26, 1835, in Wilson, 12: 394–95.

9. Benton, 550.

10. Ibid., 551.

11. J. G. deR. Hamilton, "Willie Person Mangum," 232–33; Benton, 550.

12. Benton, 553; Sears, 211. Because of Benton's persistent support for the mint bill, coins produced by the new establishments were dubbed "Benton's mint drops" (Sears, 211).

13. Head and Etheridge, 18–19, 23, 27; Clair M. Birdsall, The United States Branch Mint at Dahlonega, 7–10.

14. Annealing pans permitted slow cooling of molten gold to ensure that it would not become brittle by rapid cooling.

15. Head and Etheridge, 35.

16. Ibid., 48.

17. "Dahlonega in 1838" by an "Old Citizen," in Andrew W. Cain, History of Lumpkin County for the First Hundred Years,1832-1932, 82.

18. Birdsall, 84, 94; "Dahlonega Gold Museum"; A. S. Furcron, "A Brief History of Gold Production in Georgia," 25.

19. Paschal, 258–59.

20. "Acts of the General Assembly of the State of Georgia, 1832," 215–16.

21. "Acts of the General Assembly of the State of Georgia, 1833," 118.

22. Wilson Lumpkin, Removal of the Cherokee Indians from Georgia, 1827–1838, 1: 275.

23. Eli M'Connell to Wilson Lumpkin, May 13, 1834, in Lumpkin, 1: 274.

24. From the report of a committee headed by Howell Cobb in Cherokee County concerning the state of relations between Cherokees and whites in north Georgia, in Lumpkin, 1: 275.

25. Ibid.

26. *Western Herald*, April 23, 1833.

27. *Southern Banner*, June 1, 1833.

28. Edward E. Dale and Gaston Litton, *Cherokee Cavaliers*, 4–6.

29. Thurman Wilkins, *Cherokee Tragedy, The Ridge Family and the Decimation of a People*, 280.

30. Ibid., 286–87.

31. Theda Perdue, "The Conflict Within: The Cherokee Power Structure and Removal," 467–91.

32. Ridge's prediction proved all too accurate. On June 22, 1839, a few months after the final Cherokee removal, Major Ridge, John Ridge, and Elias Boudinot were killed by members of the Deer Clan. Wilkins, 289, 334–39.

33. Grant Foreman, *Indian Removal: The Emigration of the Five Civilized Tribes of Indians*, 299.

34. For an examination of federal action regarding Cherokee removal during this time period see Carl J. Vipperman, "The Bungled Treaty of New Echota."

35. See James F. Cook, *Governors of Georgia*.

36. Ralph Waldo Emerson, "Letter to President Van Buren," in *Complete Works*, 11: 95–96.

37. "General Scott's Address to the Cherokee," in Cain, 20–21.

38. Dale Van Every, *Disinherited: The Lost Birthright of the American Indian*, 241.

39. James Mooney, "Myths of the Cherokee," 130.

40. *Niles' Register*, January 5, 1839; Mooney, "Myths," 131; Duane H. King, "The Origin of the Eastern Cherokees as a Social and Political Entity," 172.

41. *Niles' Register*, January 5, 1839; Mooney, "Myths," 131.

42. King, 177–78. For an overview of the Eastern Band in the nineteenth century see John R. Finger, *The Eastern Band of Cherokees, 1819–1900*.

43. Van Every, 246–47.

44. *New York Observer*, January 26, 1839, in Van Every, 249–50.

45. Grace Steele Woodward, *The Cherokees*, 217–18.

46. *Sunday Oklahoman*, April 7, 1929, in Wilkins, 327.

47. George G. Ward, *The Annals of Upper Georgia*, 57.

48. Wilkins, 323, 328.

49. Report of the Lumpkin County Grand Jury, September 1838, in Cain, 68–69.

50. Van Every, 249. Van Buren was not correct, strictly speaking, when he announced the removal of the "entire" Cherokee Nation. Twenty-two of the more affluent Cherokee families were allowed to remain and were granted full citizenship under the Cherokee Indian Citizenship Act passed by the General Assembly on December 29, 1838. For a discussion of these families see Sharon Flanagan, "The Georgia Cherokees Who Remained."

51. *New York Observer,* January 26, 1839, in Van Every, 249–50.

52. Mooney, "Myths," 130.

EPILOGUE:

"Gold Fever . . . Ain't No Cure For It"

1. Southern gold mining reached its peak in the 1840s and, despite a brief resurgence in the 1850s, gradually declined to near nonexistence by the time of the Civil War. See J. T. Pardee and C. F. Park, "Gold Deposits of the Southern Piedmont," 31. One notable exception to this trend was the Gold Hill District of North Carolina. See Brent D. Glass, "Poor Men with Rude Machinery: The Formative Years of the Gold Hill Mining District, 1842–1853" and "The Miner's World: Life and Labor at Gold Hill."

2. John Kollock, *These Gentle Hills,* 36.

3. *Dahlonega Watchman,* December 21, 1848.

4. Andrew W. Cain, *History of Lumpkin County for the First Hundred Years, 1832–1932,* 106.

5. Robert B. Cook, "Minerals of Georgia," 10; W. S. Yeates, S. W. McCallie, and Francis P. King, "Gold Deposits of Georgia," 30; Clair M. Birdsall, *The Mint at Dahlonega,* 84; Sylvia Gailey Head and Elizabeth W. Etheridge, *The Neighborhood Mint,* viii.

6. Thomas Hart Benton, *Thirty Years' View,* 553.

7. G. W. Featherstonhough, *A Canoe Voyage Up the Minnay-Sotor,* 2: 303.

8. Fletcher M. Green, "Georgia's Forgotten Industry," 221–22. The attack on the branch mints was tied to an effort to recharter the Bank of the United States.

9. Head and Etheridge, viii.

10. Benton, 550.

11. *Dahlonega Nugget,* February 19, 1897; Yeates, McCallie, and King, 274–75.

12. W. R. Crandall, "The Hydraulic Elevator at the Chestatee Mine, Georgia," 62. A Georgia native, Jenny Wimmer, was the

first to identify James Marshall's find at Sutter's Mill as gold. See Donovan Lewis, "Jenny Wimmer: She Helped Discover Gold in California."

13. Norma D. Smith, *Lewis Ralston*, 4.

14. Southern Historical Association, *Memoirs of Georgia*, 2: 470. Crisson returned to Dahlonega three years later and remained there the rest of his life. The Crisson Mine is one of the few still in operation.

15. *Dahlonega Nugget*, February 19, 1897; Yeates, McCallie, and King, 274–75.

16. Cain, 106.

17. William R. Price, *Sixty Years of the Life of a Country Village Baptist Church*, 11; Yeates, McCallie, and King, 439; "Dahlonega, Georgia" (*Engineering and Mining Journal*), 170. There is some uncertainty concerning Boisclair's age at the time of his death. The 1850 census gives an age of forty-six, but the 1848 Lumpkin County Register of Free Persons of Color reads "about fifty-three year of age." The latter would place his age in 1850 at fifty-five.

18. Forest C. Wade, *Cry of the Eagle*, 79.

19. Ibid., 79–80.

20. William P. Blake and Charles T. Jackson, "Gold Placers in the Vicinity of Dahlonega," 40; "Mineral Wealth of Georgia" (*Hunt's Merchants' Magazine*).

21. T. Conn Bryan, "The Gold Rush in Georgia," *Georgia Mineral Society Newsletter*, 133–34; Elma Dill Russell Spencer, *Green Russell and Gold*, 76–77, 147.

22. William S. Kinsland, "The Dahlonega Mint: A Civil War Mystery," 39–46; F. M. Green, "Georgia's Forgotten Industry," 224–26. The mint in Charlotte also closed during the war. It was reopened in 1867 as an assay office only and functioned as such until 1913. In 1936 the building became an art museum, and it remains so to this day. See Henrietta H. Wilkinson, *The Mint Museum of Art at Charlotte*, 40, 66. The New Orleans Mint continued to coin silver into the early part of the twentieth century.

23. *Dahlonega Advertiser*, October 7, 1876. For information on gold mining in Georgia during the latter half of the nineteenth century, the best brief source is "Gold Mining in Georgia." See also Matthew F. Stephenson, "Geology and Mineralogy in Georgia," 102; J. B. Mackintosh, "The Gold Mining District of Dahlonega, Georgia"; and P. H. Mell, "Gold District of Georgia."

24. Wilber Colvin, "Gold Mining Developments in Georgia" and "Gold Mining in Georgia." See also H. V. Maxwell, "The

Crown Mountain Gold Mine and Mill"; and Edwin C. Eckel, "Gold and Pyrite Deposits of the Dahlonega District," 57–63.

25. H. V. Maxwell, "Gold Dredging in North Georgia"; Cain, 103.

26. Waldemar Lindgren, "The Production of Gold in the United States in 1904," 32.

27. *Dahlonega Nugget,* June 15, 1906. See also Lindgren, "The Gold Deposits of Dahlonega, Georgia."

28. "Southern Mining Impressions" (*Mines and Minerals*), 497.

29. For an overview of turn-of-the-century gold mining in Georgia see H. David Williams, "The Great Gold Revival: Georgia's Second Gold Rush, 1899–1906."

30. Gordon Gaskill, "A Town That Yawns at Gold."

31. *Gold Fever* (videocassette). A companion volume entitled *Gold Fever: America's First Gold Rush* is published by the Georgia Humanities Council and distributed by the University of Georgia Press. For a firsthand account of twentieth-century gold mining in Lumpkin County see Betty H. Waters, *Yarns of Gold From Auraria as told by Amy Trammell.*

32. Anne Dismukes Amerson, *I Remember Dahlonega,* 11.

33. Ibid., 19.

34. For an overview see W. Larry Otwell, *Georgia's Hidden Gold.*

Bibliography

GOVERNMENT DOCUMENTS

"Acts of the General Assembly of the State of Georgia, Passed in Milledgeville, at an Annual Session, 1826."
Milledgeville: Camak and Ragland, 1826; ibid., 1828.
Milledgeville: Camak and Ragland, 1829; ibid., 1830.
Milledgeville: Camak and Ragland, 1831; ibid., 1831.
Milledgeville: Prince and Ragland, 1832; ibid., 1832.
Milledgeville: Prince and Ragland, 1833; ibid., 1833.
Milledgeville: Polhill and Fort, 1834; ibid., 1834.
Milledgeville: P. L. and B. H. Robinson, 1835; ibid., 1837.
Milledgeville: P. L. Robinson, 1838.

"The American State Papers, Indian Affairs." Volume 2.

"An Historical Sketch of Pickens County." Works Projects Administration Project. Georgia Department of Archives and History, Atlanta.

Becker, George F. "Reconnaissance of the Gold Fields of the Southern Appalachians." U.S. Geological Survey, Sixteenth Annual Report. Washington, D.C.: Government Printing Office, 1894.

Boatright, Sherry. "The Calhoun Gold Mine: An Introductory Report on its Historical Significance." Georgia Department of Natural Resources, Atlanta, 1974.

Census of Georgia, Lumpkin County, 1834, 1838. Georgia Department of Archives and History, Atlanta.

Cook, Robert B. "Minerals of Georgia: Their Properties and Occurrences." Georgia Department of Natural Resources, Atlanta, 1978.

"Dahlonega Gold Museum." Georgia Department of Natural Resources, Atlanta, 1980.

Eckel, Edwin C. "Gold and Pyrite Deposits of the Dahlonega District, Georgia." U.S. Geological Survey, Bulletin 213. Washington, D.C.: Government Printing Office, 1902.

Funk, Linda. "The Reed Gold Mine." North Carolina Division of Archives and History, Raleigh, 1979.

"Georgia Gold." Georgia Department of Natural Resources, Atlanta.

155

"Georgia Surveyor General Department." Georgia Surveyor General Department, Atlanta.

German, Jerry. "The Geology of the Northeastern Portion of the Dahlonega Gold Belt." Georgia Geologic Survey, Bulletin 100, 1985.

Hays, Mrs. J. E., State Historian. "Indian Treaties and Cession of Land, 1705–1837." Works Project Administration, 1941. Georgia Department of Archives and History, Atlanta.

Jones, S. P. "Second Report on the Gold Deposits of Georgia." Georgia Geologic Survey, Bulletin 19, 1909.

"Journal of the House of Representatives of the State of Georgia at an Annual Session of the General Assembly Begun and Held at Milledgeville, the Seat of Government in November and December, 1828." Milledgeville: Camak and Ragland, 1828.

"Journal of the Senate of the State of Georgia at an Annual Session of the General Assembly Begun and Held at Milledgeville, the Seat of Government in November and December, 1827." Milledgeville: Camak and Ragland, 1828.

Knight, Lucian Lamar. A scrapbook of newspaper clippings on Georgia history. Georgia Department of Archives and History, Atlanta.

Liquor Selling Licenses, Court of Ordinary, Lumpkin County, Georgia, Georgia Department of Archives and History, Atlanta.

Lindgren, Waldemar. "The Production of Gold in the United States in 1904." U.S. Geological Survey, Bulletin 260. Washington, D.C.: Government Printing Office, 1905.

———. "The Gold Deposits of Dahlonega, Georgia." U.S. Geological Survey, Bulletin 293. Washington, D.C.: Government Printing Office, 1906.

McCallie, S. W. "A Preliminary Report on the Mineral Resources of Georgia." Georgia Geologic Survey, Bulletin 23, 1910.

Minutes of the Superior Court of Lumpkin County. Georgia Department of Archives and History, Atlanta.

Mooney, James. "Myths of the Cherokee." Bureau of American Ethnology, Nineteenth Annual Report, Part 1. Washington, D.C.: Government Printing Office, 1900.

———. "Sacred Formulas of the Cherokees." Bureau of American Ethnology, Seventh Annual Report. Washington, D.C.: Government Printing Office, 1888.

Pardee, J. T., and C. F. Park. "Gold Deposits of the Southern Piedmont." U.S. Geological Survey, Professional Paper No. 213. Washington, D.C.: Government Printing Office, 1948.

Raffalovich, George. "Dead Towns of Georgia." Georgia Department of Natural Resources, Atlanta, 1938.

Register of Free Persons of Color, Lumpkin County, Georgia, 1848. Georgia Department of Archives and History, Atlanta.

Royce, Charles C. "The Cherokee Nation of Indians." Bureau of American Ethnology, Fifth Annual Report, Washington, D.C.: Government Printing Office, 1887.

Stephenson, Matthew F. "Geology and Mineralogy in Georgia." Georgia Geologic Survey, 1871.

Swanton, John R. "Final Report of the United States De Soto Expedition Commission." Introduction by Jeffrey P. Brain. Washington, D.C.: Government Printing Office, 1939; reprint ed., Washington, D.C.: Smithsonian Institution Press, 1985.

United States Census, Georgia, 1850.

Yeates, W. S., S. W. McCallie, and Francis P. King. "A Preliminary Report on a Part of the Gold Deposits of Georgia." Georgia Geologic Survey, Bulletin 4-A, 1896.

PAPERS, REPORTS, AND MANUSCRIPTS

Blake, William P. "Report Upon the Property of the Mining Company called the Auraria Mines of Georgia." Boston, 1860. On microfilm reel number 186-41, Georgia Department of Archives and History, Atlanta.

————. "Prospectus of the Chestatee Hydraulic Company." New York: John F. Trow, Printer, 1858. On microfilm reel number 186-41, Georgia Department of Archives and History, Atlanta.

Blake, William P. and Charles T. Jackson. "Gold Placers in the Vicinity of Dahlonega, Georgia." Boston, 1859. On microfilm reel number 186-41, Georgia Department of Archives and History, Atlanta.

Georgia-Alabama Investment and Development Company. "Prospectus of the City of Tallapoosa, Haralson County, Georgia." Boston: The Barta Press, 1891.

Minutes of the Antioch Baptist Church in Auraria. Georgia Department of Archives and History, Atlanta.

Parks family Bible. Dahlonega Courthouse Gold Museum.

Payne, Sandra W. "Historic Tour of Pickens County." May 1977. Georgia Department of Archives and History, Atlanta.

NEWSPAPERS

Atlanta Constitution (1894, 1953, 1987).
Cherokee Phoenix, New Echota (1829, 1831–33).
Dahlonega Advertiser (1876).
Dahlonega Nugget (1897, 1906, 1917).
Dahlonega Signal (1883, 1886, 1893–94).
Dahlonega Watchman (1848).
Federal Union, Milledgeville (1832–34).
Georgia Courier, Augusta (1830–31).
Georgia Journal, Milledgeville (1829–31, 1833–34).
Georgia Messenger, Macon (1833).
Georgian, Savannah (1832, 1834–35).
Macon Advertiser (1831, 1833).
Macon Telegraph (1831)
Mountain Signal, Dahlonega (1874–75, 1880, 1882).
National Labor Tribune, Pittsburgh (1880).
Niles' Register, Baltimore (1829–33, 1839).
North Carolina Spectator, Rutherfordton (1830–31).
Southern Banner, Athens (1833–34).
Southern Recorder, Milledgeville (1826–30, 1832–33).
State Rights Sentinel, Augusta (1834–36).
Western Herald, Auraria (1833–34).

AUDIO-VISUAL MATERIAL

Gold Fever. Produced and directed by Jim Couch and Becky Marshall. 27 minutes. Georgia Department of Natural Resources,
1985. Videocassette.

THESES AND DISSERTATIONS

Glass, Brent D. "Midas and Old Rip: The Gold Hill Mining District
of North Carolina." Ph.D. dissertation, University of North
Carolina, 1980.
Vipperman, Carl. "Wilson Lumpkin and the Cherokee Removal."
Master's thesis, University of Georgia, 1961.
Wilms, Douglas C. "Cherokee Indian Land Use in Georgia, 1800–
1838." Ph.D. dissertation, University of Georgia, 1972.

BOOKS

Andrews, Garnett. *Reminiscences of an Old Georgia Lawyer*. Atlanta:
Franklin Steam Printing House, 1870.
Amerson, Anne Dismukes, ed. *I Remember Dahlonega: Memories of
Growing up in Lumpkin County as told to Anne Dismukes Amerson*.
Alpharetta, Ga.: Legacy Communications, Inc., 1990.

Benton, Thomas Hart. *Thirty Years' View, or, A History of the Working of the American Government for Thirty Years, From 1820 to 1850*. 2 vols. 1854, reprint ed., New York: Greenwood Press, 1968.

Birdsall, Clair M. *The United States Branch Mint at Dahlonega, Georgia: Its History and Coinage*. Easley, S.C.: Southern Historical Press, 1984.

Cain, Andrew W. *History of Lumpkin County for the First Hundred Years, 1832–1932*. Atlanta: Stein Printing Co., 1932; reprint ed., Spartanburg, S.C.: Reprint Co., 1984.

Cherokee County Historical Society. *Glimpses of Cherokee County*. Canton, Ga.: Industrial Printing Service, Inc., 1981.

Church, Mary L. *The Hills of Habersham*. Clarkesville, Ga.: the author, 1962.

Coleman, Kenneth, ed. *A History of Georgia*. Athens: University of Georgia Press, 1977.

Cook, James F. *Governors of Georgia*. Huntsville, Ala.: Strode Publishers, 1979.

Cooper, Ben. *Dahlonega Gold*. Atlanta: Roberts Publishing Co., 1962.

Coulter, E. Merton. *Auraria: The Story of a Georgia Gold-Mining Town*. Athens: University of Georgia Press, 1956.

——— . *George Walton Williams: The Life of a Southern Merchant and Banker, 1820–1903*. Athens: The Hibriten Press, 1976.

Crockett, David. *A Narrative of the Life of David Crockett of the State of Tennessee*. Knoxville: University of Tennessee Press, 1973.

Dale, Edward E. and Gaston Litton, eds. *Cherokee Cavaliers*. Norman: University of Oklahoma Press, 1939.

Davis, Robert Scott, Jr., and Silas Emmet Lucas, Jr. *The Georgia Land Lottery Papers, 1805–1914*. Easley, S.C.: Southern Historical Press, 1979.

Dean, Austin F., ed. *Observations from a Peak in Lumpkin, or, The Writings of W. B. Townsend, Editor, The Dahlonega Nugget*. Atlanta: Oglethorpe University Press, 1936.

Díaz, Bernal. *The Conquest of Mexico*. Middlesex, England: Penguin Books, 1963.

Emerson, Ralph Waldo. *Complete Works*. Boston: Houghton-Mifflin, 1903–04.

Fagan, Brian M. *The Great Journey: The Peopling of Ancient America*. New York: Thames and Hudson, 1987.

Featherstonhough, G. W. *A Canoe Voyage up the Minnay-Sotor, with an Account of the Lead and Copper Mines of the Gold Region in the Cherokee Country*. 2 vols. London: Richard Bentley, 1847.

Finger, John R. *The Eastern Band of Cherokees, 1819–1900*. Knoxville: University of Tennessee Press, 1984.

Foreman, Grant. *Indian Removal: The Emigration of the Five Civilized Tribes of Indians*. Norman: University of Oklahoma Press, 1953.

Gilman, Caroline. *The Poetry of Traveling in the United States*. New York: S. Colman, 1838.

Gilmer, George R. *Sketches of Some of the First Settlers of Upper Georgia, of the Cherokees, and the Author*. Americus, Ga.: Americus Book Co., 1926.

Green, Michael D. *The Politics of Indian Removal: Creek Government and Society in Crisis*. Lincoln and London: University of Nebraska Press, 1982.

Halliburton, R., Jr. *Red Over Black: Black Slavery Among the Cherokee Indians*. Westport, Conn.: Greenwood Press, 1977.

Harden, Edward J. *The Life of George M. Troup*. Savannah: E. J. Purse, 1859.

Harris, Joel Chandler. *Stories of Georgia*. New York: 1896; reprint ed., Atlanta: Cherokee Publishing Company, 1971.

Harshaw, Lou. *The Gold of Dahlonega*. Asheville, N.C.: Hexagon Company, 1976.

Head, Sylvia Gailey, and Elizabeth W. Etheridge. *The Neighborhood Mint: Dahlonega in the Age of Jackson*. Macon, Ga.: Mercer University Press, 1986.

Hepburn, A. Barton. *History of Coinage and Currency in the United States and the Perennial Contest for Sound Money*. New York: The MacMillian Company, 1903.

Heye, George G., F. W. Hodge, and George H. Pepper. *The Nacoochee Mound in Georgia*. New York: The Heye Foundation, 1918.

Hodge, Frederick W., ed. "The Narrative of Alvar Núñez Cabeca deVaca." In *Spanish Explorations in the Southern United States, 1528–1543*. New York: Charles Scribner's Sons, 1907.

Hodler, Thomas W. and Howard A. Schretter. *The Atlas of Georgia*. Athens: Institute of Community and Area Development, University of Georgia, 1986.

Inscoe, John C. *Mountain Masters, Slavery, and the Sectional Crisis in Western North Carolina*. Knoxville: University of Tennessee Press, 1989.

Jones, Charles C., Jr. *The History of Georgia*. 2 vols. Boston: Houghton, Mifflin and Company, 1883.

Kenimer, Doris Bray. *Gold in Them Thar Hills*. Gainesville, Ga.: Matthews Printing Co., 1980.

King, Duane H. "The Origin of the Eastern Cherokees as a Social and Political Entity." In *The Cherokee Indian Nation: A Troubled History*, edited by Duane H. King. Knoxville: University of Tennessee Press, 1979.

Knight, Lucian Lamar. *A Standard History of Georgia and Georgians*. Chicago and New York: Lewis Publishing Co., 1917.

———. *Georgia's Landmarks, Memorials and Legends*. Atlanta: Byrd Printing Company, 1914.

Kollock, John. *These Gentle Hills*. Lakemont, Ga.: Copple House Books, 1976.

Lanman, Charles. *Adventures in the Wilds of the United States and British American Provinces*. 2 vols. Philadelphia, 1856.

Lewis, Theodore H., ed. "The Narrative of the Expedition of Hernando de Soto, by the Gentleman of Elvas." In *Spanish Explorations in the Southern United States, 1528–1543*. New York: Charles Scribner's Sons, 1907.

Lumpkin, Wilson. *Removal of the Cherokee Indians from Georgia, 1827–1838*. 2 vols. Savannah: The Savannah Morning News Print, 1907.

Marlin, Lloyd G. *History of Cherokee County*. Atlanta: Walter W. Brown Publishing Co., 1932.

Marx, Jenifer. *The Magic of Gold*. New York: Doubleday and Co., 1978.

Moulton, Gary E. *John Ross: Cherokee Chief*. Athens: University of Georgia, 1978.

Otwell, W. Larry. *The Gold of White County, Georgia*. Cleveland, Ga.: Rainbow Sequoia, 1984.

———. *Panning Georgia's Gold*. Cleveland, Ga.: Rainbow Sequoia, 1985.

———. *Georgia's Hidden Gold: A Guide to Unexplored Ice Age Surfaces*. Cleveland, Ga.: Rainbow Sequoia, 1988.

Owsley, Frank L. *Plain Folk of the Old South*. Baton Rouge: Louisiana State University Press, 1949.

Parks, C. F., and R. A. Wilson. *The Battle Branch Gold Mine, Auraria, Georgia*. Atlanta, 1934.

Paschal, George W. *Ninety-Four Years: Agnes Paschal*. Washington, D.C., 1871; reprint ed., Spartanburg, S.C.: Reprint Co., 1974.

Perdue, Theda. *Slavery and the Evolution of Cherokee Society, 1540–1866*. Knoxville: University of Tennessee Press, 1979.

———. ed. *Cherokee Editor: The Writings of Elias Boudinot*. Knoxville: University of Tennessee Press, 1983.

Phillips, Ulrich B. *Georgia and State Rights: A Study of the Political History of Georgia from the Revolution to the Civil War, with Particular Regard to Federal Relations*. Washington, D.C.: Government Printing Office, 1902.

Price, William P. *Sixty Years of the Life of a Country Village Baptist Church*. Atlanta: Franklin Printing and Publishing Co., 1897.

Prucha, Francis Paul, ed. *Cherokee Removal: The "William Penn" Essays and Other Writings by Jeremiah Evarts*. Knoxville: University of Tennessee Press, 1981.

Remini, Robert V. *Andrew Jackson and the Course of American Freedom, 1822-1832*. New York: Harper and Row, 1981.

Rensi, Ray C., and H. David Williams. *Gold Fever: America's First Gold Rush*. Georgia History and Culture Series. Atlanta: Georgia Humanities Council, 1988.

Roberts, Bruce. *The Carolina Gold Rush: America's First*. Charlotte, N.C.: McNally and Loftin, 1982.

Roberts, Nancy. *The Gold Seekers: Gold, Ghosts and Legends from Carolina to California*. Columbia: University of South Carolina Press, 1989.

Shackford, James A. *David Crockett: The Man and the Legend*. Chapel Hill: University of North Carolina Press, 1986.

Sherwood, Adiel. *A Gazetteer of the State of Georgia*. Washington, D.C.: P. Force, 1837.

Simms, William Gilmore. *Guy Rivers: A Tale of Georgia*. New York: Harper and Brothers, 1834; reprint New York: A.M.S. Press, 1970.

Slade, M. D. J. *Prizes Drawn in the Cherokee Gold Lottery*. Milledgeville, Ga.: *The Times* Office, 1833.

Smith, James F., ed. *Cherokee Land Lottery*. New York: Harper, 1838.

Smith, Norma D. *Lewis Ralston*. Atlanta: the author, 1974.

Southern Historical Association. *Memoirs of Georgia*. 2 vols. Atlanta, 1895.

Spencer, Elma Dill Russell. *Green Russell and Gold*. Austin: University of Texas Press, 1966.

Stampp, Kenneth M. *The Peculiar Institution: Slavery in the Ante-Bellum South*. New York: Vintage Books, 1956.

Starobin, Robert S. *Industrial Slavery in the Old South*. New York: Oxford University Press, 1970.

Tate, Lucius Eugene. *History of Pickens County*. Atlanta: Walter W. Brown Pub. Co., 1935.

Taylor, George Rogers, ed. *Jackson vs. Biddle's Bank: The Struggle Over the Second Bank of the United States*. Lexington, Mass.: D. C. Heath, 1972.

Van Every, Dale. *Disinherited: The Lost Birthright of the American Indian.* New York: William Morrow and Company, 1966.

Wade, Forest C. *Cry of the Eagle: History and Legends of the Cherokee Indians and Their Buried Treasures.* Cumming, Ga.: the author, 1969.

Ward, George G. *The Annals of Upper Georgia Centered in Gilmer County.* Nashville: The Parthenon Press, 1965.

Warren, Mary Bondurant. *Alphabetical Index to Georgia's 1832 Gold Lottery.* Danielsville, Ga.: Heritage Papers, 1981.

Waters, Betty H., ed. *Yarns of Gold From Auraria as told by Amy Trammell.* Dahlonega: By the Author, 1979.

Wells, Joel Dixon. *Sixth or 1832 Land Lottery: Lists of Persons Eligible to Draw.* Hampton, Ga.: Armchair Publications, 1982.

White, George. *Historical Collections of Georgia.* New York: Pudney and Russell, Publishers, 1855.

————. *Statistics of the State of Georgia.* Savannah: W. Thorne Williams, 1849.

White County Centennial Committee. *Historical Facts and Legends of White County: 1857–1957.* Cleveland, Ga., 1957.

Wilkins, Thurman. *Cherokee Tragedy: The Ridge Family and the Decimation of a People.* Norman and London: University of Oklahoma Press, 1986.

Wilkinson, Henrietta H. *The Mint Museum of Art at Charlotte.* Charlotte, N.C.: Heritage Printers, 1973.

Wilson, Clyde N., ed. *The Papers of John C. Calhoun.* Vols. 11–13. Columbia: University of South Carolina Press, 1979.

Woodward, Grace Steele. *The Cherokees.* Norman: University of Oklahoma Press, 1963.

ARTICLES

Anderson, C. S. "Gold Mining in Georgia." *Transactions of the American Institute of Mining Engineers* 109 (1934): 61–68.

Anderson, Jimmy E. "The Life and Troubled Times of General Harrison W. Riley." *North Georgia Journal* 2 (Spring 1985): 32–41.

Bottoms, Roy E. "History of the Franklin Gold Mine." *North West Georgia Historical and Genealogical Society Quarterly* 5 (October 1973): 3–7.

Brewer, William M. "Further Notes on the Alabama and Georgia Gold Fields." *Transactions of the American Institute of Mining Engineers* 26 (1896): 464–72.

Bristol, Victor. "History of Early Settlers of Nacoochee Valley." *Georgia Pioneers Genealogical Magazine* 3 (May 1966): 66–70.

Bryan, T. Conn. "The Gold Rush in Georgia." *Georgia Review* 9 (1955): 398–404.

——— . "The Gold Rush in Georgia." *Georgia Mineral Society Newsletter* 8 (1955): 131–35.

——— . ed. "Letters Concerning Georgia Gold Mines, 1830-1834." *Georgia Historical Quarterly* 44 (1960): 338–346.

Cashin, Edward J. Review of *The Neighborhood Mint: Dahlonega in the Age of Jackson,* by Sylvia Gailey Head and Elizabeth W. Etheridge. *Georgia Historical Quarterly* 71 (1987): 514–15.

Clemson, Thomas G. "Gold and the Gold Region." *Orion* 4 (April 1844): 57–66.

Colvin, Wilber. "Gold Mining Developments in Georgia." *Engineering and Mining Journal* 71 (1901): 117–18.

——— . "Gold Mining in Georgia." *Scientific American* 83 (1900): 10-11.

Coulter, E. Merton, ed. "Reminiscences of Benjamin Franklin Matthews." *Georgia Historical Quarterly* 46 (1962): 195–207.

Covington, James W., ed. "Letters from the Georgia Gold Region." *Georgia Historical Quarterly* 39 (1955): 401–9.

Crandall, W. R. "The Hydraulic Elevator at the Chestatee Mine, Georgia." *Transactions of the American Institute of Mining Engineers* 26 (1896): 62–68.

"Dahlonega, Georgia." *Engineering and Mining Journal* 99 (January 16, 1915): 170.

"Dahlonega, or Georgia Gold Region." *Hunt's Merchants' Magazine* 19 (1848): 112–13.

Davis, Robert S. "Indians of Pickens County." *North Georgia Journal* 6 and 7 (1986): 36–38.

Flanagan, Sharon. "The Georgia Cherokees Who Remained: Race, Status, and Property in the Chattahoochee Community." *Georgia Historical Quarterly* 73 (1989): 584–609.

Fluker, W. H. "Gold Mining in McDuffie County, Georgia." *Transactions of the American Institute of Mining Engineers* 33 (1903): 119–125.

Furcron, A. S. "A Brief History of Gold Production in Georgia." *Georgia Mineral Society Newsletter* 17 (1964–1965): 24–25.

Gaskill, Gordon. "A Town That Yawns at Gold." *American Magazine* (May 1940): 16–17, 168–69.

"Georgia Gold." *American Journal of Science and Arts* 27 (1835): 255–56.

Glass, Brent D. "Poor Men with Rude Machinery: The Formative Years of the Gold Hill Mining District, 1842–1853." *North Carolina Historical Review* 61 (1984): 1–35.

————. "The Miner's World: Life and Labor at Gold Hill." *North Carolina Historical Review* 62 (1985): 420–47.

Goad, Sharon I. "Copper and the Southeastern Indians." *Early Georgia* 4 (1976): 48–67.

"Gold in Maryland." *American Journal of Science and Arts* 17 (1830): 202.

"Gold Mines of North Carolina." *American Journal of Science and Arts* 16 (1829): 360–63.

"Gold Mining in Georgia." *Harper's New Monthly Magazine* 59 (1879): 506–19.

"Gold Region of the United States." *American Journal of Science and Arts* 7 (1835): 348–51.

Green, Fletcher M. "Georgia's Forgotten Industry: Gold Mining." *Georgia Historical Quarterly* 19 (1935): 91–111, 210–28.

————. "Gold Mining: A Forgotten Industry of Ante-Bellum North Carolina." *North Carolina Historical Review* 14 (1937): 1–19, 135–55.

————. "Gold Mining in Ante-Bellum Virginia." *The Virginia Magazine of History and Biography* 45 (1937): 227–35, 357–66.

Hamilton, J. G. deR. "Willie Person Mangum." In *Dictionary of American Biography.* Edited by Allen Johnson. New York: Charles Scribner's Sons, 1929, 12: 232–33.

Hutchins, John. "The Trial of Reverend Samuel A. Worcester." *Journal of Cherokee Studies* (Fall 1977): 356–74.

Kinsland, William S. "The Dahlonega Mint: A Civil War Mystery." *North Georgia Journal* 1 (Summer 1984): 39–46.

Knapp, Richard F. "Golden Promise in the Piedmont: The Story of John Reed's Mine." *North Carolina Historical Review* 52 (1975): 1–19.

Lewis, Donovan. "Jenny Wimmer: She Helped Discover Gold in California." *True West* (July 1984): 21–25.

Mackintosh, J. B. "The Gold Mining District of Dahlonega, Georgia." *Engineering and Mining Journal* 27 (1879): 258.

Maxwell, H. V. "The Crown Mountain Gold Mine and Mill, Georgia." *Engineering and Mining Journal* (September 21, 1901): 355–56.

————. "Gold Dredging in North Georgia." *Engineering and Mining Journal* (November 2, 1901).

McCallie, S. W. "The Gold Deposits of Georgia." *Georgia Mineral Society Newsletter* 3 (1950): 32–33, and 4 (1951): 59–61, 106–7, 152–55, 172–74. From notebook MC–5, "The Gold Deposits of Georgia and Road Data, 1895–1898," Georgia Geologic Survey.

McLoughlin, William G. "Georgia's Role in Instigating Compulsory Indian Removal." *Georgia Historical Quarterly* 70 (1986): 605-32.

McRay, Sybil. "Paschal Family Tree." *North Georgia Journal* 6 & 7 (1986): 85–86.

Mell, P. H. "Gold District of Georgia." *Engineering and Mining Journal* 24 (1877): 528.

"Mineral Wealth of Georgia." *Hunt's Merchants' Magazine* 36 (1857): 632–33.

"Mining Interest at the South." *Russell's Magazine* 3 (1858): 442–47.

"Miscellanies." *American Journal of Science and Arts* 20 (1831): 401–3.

Mitchell, Larry E. "Benjamin Parks: A Really Golden Heritage." *North Georgia Journal* 2 (Spring 1985): 16–29.

Olmsted, Denison. "On the Gold Mines of North Carolina." *American Journal of Science and Arts* 9 (1825): 5–15.

Park, C. F., Jr. "Gold Deposits of Georgia." *Georgia Mineral Society Newsletter* 6 (1953): 107–113.

Peck, Jacob. "Geological and Mineralogical Account of the Mining Districts in the State of Georgia–Western Part of North Carolina and of East Tennessee." *American Journal of Science and Arts* 23 (1833): 1–10.

Perdue, Theda. "The Conflict Within: The Cherokee Power Structure and Removal." *Georgia Historical Quarterly* 73 (1989): 467–991.

Peyton, Garland. "The Old-Time Stamp Mill." *Georgia Mineral Society Newsletter* 4 (1951): 93–95.

Phifer, Edward W., Jr. "Champagne at Brindletown: The Story of the Burke County Gold Rush, 1829–1833." *North Carolina Historical Review* 40 (1963): 489–500.

Phillips, William. "Essay on the Georgia Gold Mines." *American Journal of Science and Arts* 24 (1833): 1–18.

Richardson, L. W. "Templeton Reid: Early Georgia Coin Maker." *North Georgia Journal* 1 (Summer 1984): 31–38.

Rothe, Charles E. "Remarks on the Gold Mines of North Carolina." *American Journal of Science and Arts* 13 (1828): 201–17.

Russell, Robert A. "Gold Mining in Alabama Before 1860." *Alabama Review* 10 (1957): 5–14.

Sears, Louis S. "Thomas Hart Benton." In *Dictionary of American Biography.* Edited by Allen Johnson. New York: Charles Scribner's Sons, 1929, 2: 210–213.

Seymour, Dexter C. "Templeton Reid, First of the Pioneer Coiners." *The American Numismatic Society Museum Notes* 19 (1974): 225–67.

Smith, Marvin T. "The Route of De Soto Through Tennessee, Georgia, and Alabama: The Evidence from Material Culture." *Early Georgia* 4 (September 1976): 27–47.

"Southern Mining Impressions." *Mines and Minerals* (June 1903): 495–97.

"Statistics of Coinage." *Hunt's Merchants' Magazine* 4 (1841): 382–87.

Sturtevant, William C., ed. "John Ridge on Cherokee Civilization in 1826." *Journal of Cherokee Studies* (Fall 1981): 79–91.

Vipperman, Carl J. "The Bungled Treaty of New Echota: The Failure of Cherokee Removal, 1836–1838." *Georgia Historical Quarterly* 73 (1989): 540–58.

Williams, H. David. "Agnes Paschal: The Angel of Auraria." *North Georgia Journal* 6 and 7 (1986): 80–85.

———. "Origins of the North Georgia Gold Rush." *Proceedings and Papers of the Georgia Association of Historians* (1988): 161–68.

———. "Gambling Away the Inheritance: The Cherokee Nation and Georgia's Gold and Land Lotteries of 1832–1833." *The Georgia Historical Quarterly* 73 (1989): 519–39.

———. "Georgia's Forgotten Miners: African-Americans and the Georgia Gold Rush." *Georgia Historical Quarterly* 75 (1991): 76–89.

———. "The Great Gold Revival: Georgia's Second Gold Rush, 1899–1906." *Atlanta History: A Journal of Georgia and the South* 35 (Fall 1991): 31–41.

Wilms, Douglas C. "Georgia's Land Lottery of 1832." *Chronicles of Oklahoma* 52 (1974): 52–60.

Young, Mary. "Racism in Red and Black: Indians and Other Free People of Color in Georgia Law, Politics, and Removal Policy." *Georgia Historical Quarterly* 73 (1989): 492–518.

Young, Otis E., Jr. "The Southern Gold Rush, 1828–1836." *The Journal of Southern History* 48 (August 1982): 373–92.

Index

Stephens, Joel, 23
Stephenson, Matthew, 118
Strother, Martin, 78
Stroup, Jacob, 63
Stuart, Thomas, 129 n.49
Summerall, Allen, 55
Sumter, T. W. A., 68
Sutter's Mill, 151–52 n.12
Sweden, 88
Switzerland, 88

Tassels, Corn (George Tassels), 41,
    134 n.19
Tate, Samuel, 58
Tate, Ga., 58, 137 n.41
Tattnall County, 55
Tennessee, state of, 14, 38, 40, 58,
    100; miners from, 69, 89; traders
    from, 80, 91
Tennessee River, 114
Thompson Mine. *See* Gold mining
    in Georgia
Towns, Benjamin, 107
Townsend, W. B., 140 n.6
Trail of Tears, 4, 110, 112–15, 122
Trammell, Amy, 122
Treaty of Holston, 13
Treaty of Hopewell, 13
Treaty of Indian Springs, 13–14
Treaty of New Echota, 110–12, 114
Treaty of Washington (1826), 14
Treaty Party, 111–12
Troup, George M., 13–14, 18, 99
Troup Party, 99
Tsali, 113–14
Twain, Mark, 118
Twenty-niners. *See* Gold miners in
    Georgia

Underwood, John, 21
Underwood, Judge William H.,
    40, 41, 46, 108, 130 n.16, 134
    n.19
Union County, 58
Union Party, 99, 147 n.93

United States, Bank of the, 80,
    105, 106

Van Buren, Martin, 112, 115, 148–
    49 n.7
Vann, David, 50
Vann, Joseph, 111
Villa Rica, Ga. (Hixville,
    Hixtown), 12, 28, 64
Virginia, state of, 3, 10, 12, 14,
    25, 39

Wager, Phillip, 32, 33, 130 n.28,
    132 nn. 74, 77
Waggamon, George A., 106
Wales, 88
Wales, Samuel N., 25
Walker, Isaac R., 61
Walton County, 60
Ware, John H., 94
Ware and Matthews Mining Com-
    pany, 77
Washington, George, 41
Washington County, 9
Wasitani, 113
Watie, Stand, 111
Watkins, Robert A., 87
White, C. P., 106
White, William, 130 n.16
White County, 8, 9, 21, 58, 71, 74,
    121, 138 n.74. *See also* Duke's
    Creek; Loudsville; Nacoochee
White Path Mine. *See* Gold mining
    in Georgia
Wiles, D. A., 94
Williams, Edward, 84
Williams, George, 84
Williams Mine. *See* Gold mining
    in Georgia
Wimmer, Jenny, 151–52 n.12
Winfrey, R. R., 62
Wirt, William, 40–44
Witheroods, John, 21–22
Witherow, Alfred, 85
Witherow, Jefferson, 85
Witherow, John, 21–22